The International
TOFU
Cookery Book

THE AUTHOR

Born in the USA, Leah Leneman has lived in Britain for the past twenty years. She spent several years working for British Airways, and travelled extensively. She has been Assistant Editor of *The Vegetarian*, and now writes vegetarian cookery books and articles on a freelance basis. Her previous books include *Slimming the Vegetarian Way (1980)*, *Vegan Cooking* (1982) and *The Amazing Avocado* (1984).

Illustrations by
Megan Dickinson

The International

TOFU

Cookery Book

LEAH LENEMAN

ROUTLEDGE & KEGAN PAUL

London and New York

First published in 1986
by Routledge & Kegan Paul plc
11 New Fetter Lane, London EC4P 4EE
Published in the USA by
Routledge & Kegan Paul Inc.
in association with Methuen Inc.
29 West 35th Street, New York, NY 10001

Set in Palatino 10/11½pt.
by Columns of Reading
and printed in Great Britain
by The Guernsey Press Co. Ltd.
Guernsey, Channel Islands
©Leah Leneman 1986

Library of Congress Cataloging in Publication Data

Leneman, Leah.
The international tofu cookery book.
Includes index.
1. Cookery (Tofu)   I. Title.
TX814.5.T63L46   1986   641.6'5655   85-19378

ISBN 0-7102-0702-6 (pbk.)

Contents

Introduction

Tofu – also known as soya bean curd – has been a staple food of the Orient for centuries. In recent years it has been growing in popularity in the West to a phenomenal extent. There are several reasons for this.

The first is its nutritional advantages. The modern Western diet, which is high in saturated animal fats and cholesterol, is strongly implicated in obesity and heart disease; many people are seeking alternatives. Tofu is high in protein, yet low in calories and free of cholesterol. Puréed, it can provide rich creamy substitutes for mayonnaise, soured cream, whipped cream and other dairy products, with a fraction of the calories. Mashed, it can be used in place of eggs with none of the cholesterol content. And, deep-fried or sautéed, it can provide the same service for dishes normally containing meat, fish or chicken.

Anyone tasting tofu for the first time is surprised at how bland it is, but it is this blandness which is one of its greatest assets since it can absorb any kind of flavouring. And, unlike soya beans themselves, which can cause flatulence, tofu is very easy to digest, and can be eaten even by young children or the elderly with no harmful consequences.

Another reason for tofu's growing popularity is its cost, which for such a high-quality food – manufactured at present in comparatively small quantities – is very low. For the *full* benefit of tofu's low cost, though, one really needs to make tofu at home.

Another reason why more and more people are trying tofu is compassion. The public is gradually becoming aware of the full horrors of factory farming, and slowly realising that even a lacto-vegetarian diet, which avoids slaughterhouse products, does not go far enough. The enforced continued lactation of cows, the separation of calf from cow (the former to the veal pen, the latter to produce milk for human consumption), and the battery cage are all part of the system. Cutting down on, or giving up, such cruelty-laden foods is made much easier with the use of soya milk and tofu.

Not only animals, but human beings all over the globe would benefit from the change, for at present a large proportion of the world's soya bean crop is fed to animals, an extremely inefficient use of global resources. Indeed, if the protein available from the soya bean crop grown today – let alone the additional amount which could be grown if more land were released from grazing livestock – were utilized directly by human beings, a large percentage of the world's protein deficiency could be wiped out tomorrow. It should be emphasized that, unlike TVP-type meat substitutes, which require a fairly sophisticated technology, tofu is simple enough to be made in any home.

Of course, tofu sales would not be growing by such leaps and bounds were altruism the sole motive. People may care about their health, about animals, or about the world food problem, but few of them would care enough to go on buying ever-increasing amounts of tofu unless they actually *liked* it. Tofu is fun – it can be used in more interesting and varied ways than any other single food. Basically, the cook who can get tired of tofu must be tired of life.

Types of tofu
readily available

There are basically three types of tofu, further details of which are given below. Silken tofu is very soft; medium tofu is firmer (you could lift a square of it but would need to be careful as it is still delicate and a piece could break off); firm tofu can be held up as a block without fear of breakage.

Morinaga silken tofu

As a 'long-life' product which does not require refrigeration, this variety of tofu can be found in most health food stores. It is slightly firmer than traditional silken tofu, and it can be firmed up still further by wrapping it in a tea towel to extract as much water as possible. However, whatever the manufacturers may claim, it is actually very difficult to use this product in place of medium or firm tofu; if cubed the pieces are prone to disintegrate and if mashed the fluid content is too great for a firm texture to be achieved. I have therefore specified this tofu in only a few recipes where I myself have found it satisfactory.

Japanese instant silken tofu

Anyone wandering around a Chinese supermarket may have come across these boxes of do-it-yourself 'House' tofu, containing soya milk powder and a coagulant. Those who have bought it and followed the instructions will have found themselves with quite a large quantity of very soft tofu, not easy to use. However, see 'Converted Japanese tofu' below.

Medium tofu

If you make your own tofu using epsom salts or lemon juice then you are likely to have medium tofu (particularly if you do not press it for too long). If you buy fresh homemade tofu at a wholefood shop it may also be medium tofu. However, most commercially produced tofu in this country is vacuum-packed to preserve freshness, and all of the vacuum-packed varieties I have tried are in the 'firm' category. Medium tofu is therefore the least readily available in the UK, except the Chinese kind (see below). Medium tofu is more commonly found in the USA.

Chinese tofu

Chinese supermarkets in many large towns and cities sell blocks of fresh tofu. Chinese tofu is of a 'medium' texture. However, the coagulant used for Chinese tofu produces a distinctive flavour which makes it unsuitable for many recipes, particularly sweet recipes, though naturally it is fine for Oriental dishes.

Converted Japanese tofu

By following the instructions on a packet of Japanese 'House' tofu but using only 2/3 pint (1½ US cups) of water, a medium tofu can be made. Immediately after adding the coagulant and stirring the mixture, pour it into a container, cover it and leave until cool. Then slide a knife round the sides, fill the container with water, cover again and refrigerate until needed. The texture will be similar to Chinese tofu (though I do not find it as satisfactory for deep-frying), but the taste is totally different, being quite sweet.

Because of its taste and texture I have found converted Japanese tofu ideal for recipes – both savoury and sweet – which would normally call for a milk custard. NB. One packet prepared in this way will yield approximately 12 ounces of tofu. (The curds and whey are not separated.)

Firm tofu

At the time of writing, the following all manufacture high-quality vacuum-packed firm tofu, available in various parts of the country.
Cauldron Foods, 149A South Liberty Lane, Ashton Vale, Bristol.
The Regular Tofu Co., 16 The Halfcroft, Syston, Leicester.
Paul's Tofu (organic), The Old Brewery, Wheathampstead House, Wheathampstead, St Albans, Herts.
Bean Machine, Station Road, Crymych, Dyfed.

It would be rare indeed to find a health food store in the USA that did *not* stock fresh tofu, and in most large American cities tofu is even available in supermarkets. There would therefore be little point in listing suppliers. All of the varieties described above are available in the USA; however, unlike the UK, medium rather than firm tofu is more commonly found. If medium tofu is well drained, then wrapped in a towel, and a weight placed on it for at least 20 minutes to expel some of the moisture, then it will be close to firm tofu in texture.

I have specified, in order of preference, the kind of tofu I found suitable for each recipe, but other cooks may decide they like a different texture entirely.

More unusual forms of tofu

Fermented tofu

This can be found in jars and tins at Chinese supermarkets.
Fermented tofu is said to be a bit like Camembert cheese,
but the salt concentration is much too high for it to be
palatable on its own. It does, however, add a pleasant,
distinctive flavour to a tofu dip, as in the following recipe.

Tofu dip with fermented Tofu

1 packet Morinaga silken tofu
2 tablespoons vegetable oil
2-3 cubes fermented tofu

2 teaspoons lemon juice
Blend all ingredients
 thoroughly in a liquidizer.

Dried-frozen tofu

Ordinary tofu can be frozen; when thawed it will have a
'meatier' consistency than when fresh. Dried-frozen tofu –
which is very convenient as it can be kept in the larder for
emergency use at any time – is available at some wholefood
shops and through Clearspring Natural Grocer, 196 Old
Street, London EC1V 9BP.

A 3½ oz packet will make four servings. To rehydrate the

squares put them in a large bowl and pour plenty of boiling water over them. After about five minutes pour off the water and add cold water. Take out each square and press it firmly between the palms of the hands to expel as much water as possible. The easiest way to prepare it then is simply to dip the slices into arrowroot or cornflour, or alternatively into soya milk and then breadcrumbs, and then deep-fry (or sauté) the slices until browned and crisp. Served with lemon juice or tomato ketchup (and if you want to be really traditional, peas and chips), it makes a remarkably good fried 'fish'.

Deep-fried tofu

Some Chinese shops sell tofu which has already been deep-fried, though this tends to be sold in rather large quantities. The difference in water content between Chinese (medium) and firm tofu becomes really obvious if you deep-fry your own: 12 ounces of Chinese tofu will yield about 5 ounces of deep-fried tofu, while 12 ounces of firm tofu will yield about 9 ounces of deep-fried tofu. If done properly – i.e. at the right temperature – deep-frying is not at all unhealthy, as very little oil is actually absorbed by the tofu. To deep-fry tofu, one should either invest in a cooking thermometer and heat the oil to 350°F (180°C) before lowering the tofu cubes into the oil, or alternatively use a deep-fat fryer, which automatically regulates the temperature required for this purpose.

Bean curd sticks or sheets

These can be found in Chinese supermarkets and are used in Chinese cuisine to produce delicacies like 'mock duck'. However, in spite of what they are called, they are not actually tofu at all; they are made from the skin which is skimmed off in the making of soya milk. This being the case – added to the fact that they are rather a specialist food and also that there is such a multitude of dishes to be created from ordinary tofu – I decided to exclude them from this book.

General notes

The addition of the word '-style' to every type of cuisine feature in this book is quite deliberate. I make no pretence that the recipes are necessarily 'authentic'. They were adapted by me using ingredients which were obtainable and which I liked.

Where a particular ingredient might be unfamiliar to some readers (e.g. sesame oil or yellow bean paste) I have tried to indicate where this can be found. It may be worth mentioning that I do not live in, or near, London: large towns and cities in Britain and the USA are becoming increasingly well stocked with ethnic foods.

Quantities

All the recipes in this book are meant to be self-contained dishes to serve four people for lunch or dinner (with perhaps a sweet to follow). Desserts are also meant to serve four. Naturally, appetites vary a great deal, and so do menus – if you serve soup or an appetizer, side dishes or salads, then the recipes would probably feed more. Blocks of tofu come in diverse weights, and homemade tofu also varies in weight, so I have tried to give a 'spread' of acceptable amounts for most recipes.

Tofu mayonnaise

Creamy tofu salad dressings are being manufactured by two

or three soyfood companies. At time of writing the most readily available is 'Duchesse Tofu Dressing and Dip' (made by St Giles Foods Ltd, St Giles House, Sandhurst Road, Sidcup, Kent DA15 7HL). Tofu mayonnaise is easy enough to concoct; for an example see the recipe for Potato salad on p. 22.

Soya yogurt

This is not something you can find in shops (yet), but it is very simple to make. Use powdered ferment, which is available at health food stores, and any commercially available soya milk. (Powdered or concentrated soya milks do have one advantage over ready-to-use varieties in cartons: the quantity of water can be varied to produce a thicker or thinner yogurt, depending on its intended use.) Bring the soya milk to the boil, then cool it to just above lukewarm, and follow the instructions on the packet of ferment. A wide-rimmed vacuum flask is really as effective as a yogurt-maker for the purpose. The first batch or two of soya yogurt is never very flavourful, but if you keep using a spoonful of soya yogurt to make the next batch, it gets better and better, and it will keep going for many months before a new packet of ferment is required.

American measurements

The quantities in brackets are American 8-ounce cups (not British cups, which are 10 fluid ounces). American cooks should note that British spoon measurements are about one-quarter larger than American, and adjust quantities accordingly.

Making tofu at home

The method below does not necessarily make the smoothest tofu, nor the greatest quantity. It does, however, make a delicious firm tofu, and it is so much quicker and easier than any other method I have read about I can't imagine making it any other way.

In order to make tofu the following are required: a large saucepan (holding at least 6 pints), a liquidizer, a colander, a small box (about 6in × 4in (150 × 100mm)) with small holes punched in the bottom and sides (the holes can be punched into an ordinary plastic sandwich box, and the sides cut off the lid so it fits in on top), a large piece of muslin (about 2 ft (¾ m)) and a small piece of muslin (to fit inside the box). If you are making tofu to be mashed or puréed rather than sliced or cubed, you can omit the box and just use a colander lined with muslin.

There are various coagulants which can be used to curdle the soya milk, the commonest being lemon juice, epsom salts, and a seawater product called 'nigari'. Any of these are all right, but the most strongly recommended is nigari, for three reasons: (1) it makes the firmest tofu, (2) it makes the best-tasting tofu, and (3) it is virtually foolproof. Nigari is becoming much more readily available at wholefood shops, but anyone unable to get hold of it can order it by post from Sunwheel Foods, 196 Old Street, London EC1V 9BP or from Real Foods, 37 Broughton St, Edinburgh.

The night before, cover half a pound of soya beans with boiling water and leave them to soak. In the morning drain and rinse. Place a cupful of the soaked beans in the liquidizer, add a cupful of cold water and liquidize. Then add about 2 cupfuls of boiling water to the liquidizer and liquidize again. NB. If your liquidizer is not large enough then a smaller quantity can be done each time as long as the proportions are kept more or less the same – it is *not* necessary to measure with any great precision when making tofu.

Place the large piece of muslin over the saucepan and carefully pour the contents of the liquidizer into it. Pull up the sides to make it into a sack so that the soya milk runs through, and squeeze gently to get all of the liquid into the saucepan. (The pulp left in the muslin is called 'okara' and can be used in savouries; it is high in protein but, unlike tofu, is not very easy to digest.)

Once all of the beans have been used up put the saucepan onto a medium to high heat and bring to the boil, stirring the bottom from time to time. Keep a careful eye on it because it can boil over very suddenly and dramatically. As soon as it is at the boil turn the heat down very low so it is still simmering but no longer threatening to erupt. Leave it to simmer for about three minutes.

Meanwhile, put a heaped teaspoon of nigari or other coagulant into a teacup. Fill it half full of boiling water and stir well. Remove the soya milk from the heat, then gently stir in the dissolved coagulant, trying to make certain it has been stirred through all of the liquid. Leave for about three minutes, by which time curds should have formed.

Place the muslin-lined box (if used) in the colander, then gradually pour the contents of the saucepan into it, so that the whey runs through and the curds settle in the box. Then put the colander over the empty saucepan to continue to drain, and place something heavy (about 2lb) on top. Leave for an hour or so before unmoulding. Half a pound of soya beans will make about 12 oz of tofu (though it can vary by 2 oz either way).

If the tofu is not to be used immediately it should be stored in the refrigerator in an airtight container of water, where it will keep for about a week. (Most instructions tell you to change the water every day, but if the container is left undisturbed then this really is not necessary.)

If the tofu has been stored and is to be sautéed or deep-fried rather than mashed or puréed it is best to drain it thoroughly first and then wrap it in a tea towel for a short while to get rid of surplus water. Deep-fried tofu will keep for several days longer in the fridge; store the cubes dry, in a polythene bag. (For instructions on deep-frying tofu see p. 7.)

Soya flour tofu

Whisk one part of soya flour into three parts boiling water. Simmer for 15-20 minutes, stirring occasionally. Add approximately 1 teaspoon coagulant per quart of liquid and proceed as above. Do not expect the result to be the same as when using soya beans. The curd will be much smaller, and no matter how long you press it, soya flour tofu never becomes firm enough to sauté or deep-fry. It can, however, be used in recipes requiring mashed or puréed tofu.

Soya milk tofu

Any of the commercial soya milks can be curdled to make tofu. Bring the milk to the boil, then remove from heat and add coagulant (about a teaspoon per quart of milk). The texture will be similar to that of soya flour tofu and not suitable for frying.

Table of metric equivalents

One ounce is equivalent to 28 grams, which can add up to very awkward amounts if used literally. Below is a simplified table of equivalents for those who prefer to weigh things metrically.

1 oz = 25 gm	11 oz = 300 gm
2 oz = 50 gm	12 oz = 350 gm
3 oz = 75 gm	13 oz = 375 gm
4 oz = 100 gm	14 oz = 400 gm
5 oz = 150 gm	15 oz = 425 gm
6 oz = 175 gm	1 lb = 450 gm
7 oz = 200 gm	
8 oz = 225 gm	½ pint = 275 ml
9 oz = 250 gm	1 pint = 575 ml
10 oz = 275 gm	

British- and American-style dishes

1
Substantial salads

Shredded vegetable and brown rice salad with miso dressing

12 oz (2 cups) brown rice
2 large or 4-5 small spring
 onions
1 large or 2 small cloves garlic
2 tablespoons minced parsley
½ teaspoon dry mustard
Juice of ½ lemon
8 tablespoons vegetable oil
3 tablespoons cider vinegar
1 heaped tablespoon miso

2 tablespoons honey
3 tablespoons water
2 small or 1 large potato
2 small or 1 large tomato
1 stick celery
3 oz white cabbage
4 oz raw beetroot
3 oz alfalfa sprouts
4 oz (½ cup) deep-fried tofu
 (small cubes) (see p. 7)

Cook the brown rice and cool. Mince the spring onions and garlic finely. Combine them with the parsley, mustard, lemon juice, half the oil and vinegar, and mix well with the rice. Leave to marinate in a cool place or fridge for at least an hour.

Combine the remainder of the oil and vinegar with the miso, honey and water in a liquidizer and blend thoroughly. Set aside.

Cook the potatoes until tender. Cool. Chop the tomatoes, celery and potatoes. Grate the cabbage and beetroot. Combine with the alfalfa sprouts and tofu in a large bowl, and pour the miso dressing over it. Mix thoroughly.

Use the marinated rice as a base and top with the vegetables and tofu in miso dressing.

Curried cauliflower and tofu salad

8 oz (1⅓ cups) brown rice
1 small cauliflower
1 tablespoon vegetable oil
1 tablespoon cider vinegar
4 tablespoons tofu mayonnaise
  (see p. 9)
2 tablespoons soya milk
1 tablespoon curry powder

Sea salt & freshly ground
  black pepper
8-10 oz (1-1¼ cups) firm tofu,
  deep-fried
2 small green peppers
2 sticks celery
1 small onion
1 lettuce

Cook the brown rice and cool.

Wash and dry the cauliflower and divide it into small sprigs. Mix the rice with the oil and vinegar and the cauliflower and set aside.

Combine the tofu mayonnaise, soya milk, curry powder, and salt and pepper in a large bowl, add the cubes of deep-fried tofu, and mix thoroughly.

Slice the green pepper into thin strips. Chop the celery. Mince the onion.

Combine the rice mixture, the tofu mixture, and the chopped vegetables, and serve on a bed of lettuce.

Brown rice and sweetcorn salad

8 oz (1⅓ cups) brown rice
1 green or red pepper
2 large or 4-6 small spring
  onions

8 black olives
1 14-oz tin sweetcorn
2 teaspoons dried basil (or 2
  tablespoons chopped fresh)

8 oz (1 cup) firm tofu
2 teaspoons soya sauce
½ teaspoon dried mustard
2 tablespoons cider vinegar
2 tablespoons lemon juice

4 tablespoons olive oil
Freshly ground black pepper
Lettuce leaves
2 tomatoes

Cook the rice until tender, then cool.

Chop the pepper. Mince the spring onions and olives. Combine the rice with the sweetcorn, spring onions, olives and basil. Crumble the tofu into this mixture.

Combine soya sauce, mustard, vinegar, lemon juice, oil and pepper, and stir well with a fork.

Add the dressing to the rice mixture and mix thoroughly. Leave to marinate for at least an hour in a cool place or fridge.

Slice the tomatoes. Serve the salad piled on to lettuce leaves and garnish with tomatoes.

Rice and bulghur wheat salad with tofu dressing

6 oz (1 cup) brown rice
1 onion
2 tablespoons vegetable oil
1 pint (2½ cups) vegetable
  stock
1-2 teaspoons soya sauce
2 cloves garlic
4 oz (¾ cup) bulghur wheat
2 tablespoons lemon juice

Sea salt to taste
12 oz (1½ cups) Silken tofu
2 tablespoons cider vinegar
1 tablespoon sesame oil
2 tablespoons soya sauce
2 tablespoons minced parsley
3-4 spring onions
Lettuce leaves

Cover the rice with boiling water, cover with a lid and leave to soak for several hours. Drain.

Chop the onion finely. Sauté in the vegetable oil until lightly browned. Stir in the rice, add stock and soya sauce, bring to the boil, and simmer for 10-15 minutes.

Crush the garlic. Stir the bulghur wheat, lemon juice, garlic and salt into the rice, and simmer for about 10 minutes longer, until both rice and bulghur wheat are tender and the liquid is absorbed.

Put the tofu and the next 4 ingredients into a liquidizer and purée thoroughly. Mince the spring onions and stir into the dressing.

Pour the dressing over the rice and wheat, and stir well. Leave to cool, or chill in fridge, and serve piled on lettuce leaves.

Creamy brown rice salad
with marinated vegetables

10 oz (1⅔ cups) brown rice
8 oz fresh or frozen green
  beans
2 medium carrots
2 medium or 3 small cour-
  gettes (zucchini)
¼ cup olive oil
2 tablespoons cider vinegar
¼ teaspoon dry mustard

Sea salt and freshly ground
  black pepper to taste
1 small onion
6 oz (¾ cup) medium or soft
  tofu
8 oz (1⅓ cups) thick soya
  yogurt (see p. 10)
2 cloves garlic
Juice of ½ lemon

Cook the rice until tender and leave to cool.

Slice the beans thinly and parboil until just tender. Drain. Dice the carrots and courgettes.

Combine the oil, vinegar, mustard and a little salt and pepper. Mince the onion and add it to the mixture, along with the beans, courgettes and carrots. Mix thoroughly, cover and refrigerate for several hours.

Put the tofu, yogurt, garlic, and lemon juice in a liquidizer and blend thoroughly. Add salt and pepper to taste.

Combine the rice with the tofu mixture. Put it on a serving platter (or individual plates) and top with the vegetable mixture.

Brown rice, tofu and green pepper salad

10 oz (1⅔ cups) brown rice
10-12 oz (1¼-1½ cups)
   medium or soft tofu or 1
   packet Morinaga silken tofu
4 spring onions
1 large green pepper
2 tablespoons minced parsley

4 tablespoons vegetable oil
2 tablespoons lemon juice or
   cider vinegar
½ teaspoon garlic salt
Lettuce leaves and tomatoes as
   required.

Cook the rice until tender, cool and then chill.

Mash the tofu. Mince the spring onions. Slice the green pepper thinly. Add these ingredients to the rice along with the parsley and mix well.

Combine the oil, lemon juice or vinegar, and garlic salt, and add to the rice mixture, mixing in thoroughly.

Serve on lettuce leaves, garnished with sliced tomatoes.

*Potato salad with tofu dressing**

8-12 oz (1-1½ cups) medium tofu or 1 packet Morinaga silken tofu
1-2 tablespoons lemon juice or cider vinegar

2 tablespoons vegetable oil
Sea salt and freshly ground black pepper to taste
1½-2 lb potatoes
1 large onion

Put the tofu, lemon juice or vinegar, oil and seasoning into the liquidizer and blend thoroughly.

Cook the potatoes until tender, then peel if desired. Slice them.

Mince the onion.

While they are still warm, mix the potatoes with the onion and dressing.

Chill before serving.

*This recipe previously appeared in *The Vegetarian*, Sept/Oct 1982.

2
Main dishes

Baked stuffed aubergines

2 large or 4 small aubergines
  (eggplants)
Sea salt as required
4 tablespoons olive oil
1 onion
1 garlic clove
1 oz (⅛ cup) vegetable
  margarine

12 oz mushrooms
Freshly ground black pepper
6 oz (¾ cup) firm tofu
2 tablespoons minced parsley
½ teaspoon dried thyme
1 14-oz tin tomatoes
1-2 teaspoons basil or
  marjoram

Slice the aubergines in half lengthways. With a sharp knife make cuts in the flesh to within ¼-inch of the skin. Sprinkle the aubergines with sea salt, turn them cut side down on to kitchen towels and leave them for half an hour.

Rinse and squeeze the aubergines to remove as much liquid as possible and dry them. Place them, skin side down, on a grill pan, and sprinkle each half with a teaspoon of olive oil. Place the dish under a moderate grill and grill for about 10 minutes until the flesh is soft.

Scoop the flesh from the aubergines, leaving the skins intact. Roughly chop it and set it aside.

Chop the onion finely and crush the garlic. Heat the remaining olive oil in a large frying pan over moderate heat. Add the onion and garlic, and sauté for a few minutes until the onion is tender but not brown. Chop the mushrooms.

Add the margarine to the frying pan, and when it has melted add the mushrooms. Cook for a few more minutes, until the mushrooms are tender.

Remove the pan from the heat. Stir in the chopped aubergine flesh and black pepper to taste. Crumble the tofu into the mixture, with the parsley and thyme. Mix well.

Fill the aubergine shells with the tofu and mushroom mixture. Place them in an oiled baking dish and cover it tightly with aluminium foil. Bake at 400°F (200°C) Gas Mark 6, for 25 minutes. Uncover and bake for a further 5 minutes.

Meanwhile, liquidize the tomatoes with the herb, and heat in a small saucepan. Serve the aubergines with the tomato sauce poured over them. Nice with a crisp green salad.

Tofu à la king

4 oz mushrooms
Half a green pepper
12 oz (1½ cups) firm tofu
4 oz (½ cup) vegetable
  margarine
1½ oz (⅔ cup) wholemeal flour

¾ pint (2 cups) soya milk
Sea salt, freshly ground black
  pepper, paprika or ground
  nutmeg
Buttered wholemeal toast or
  noodles

Slice the mushrooms. Chop the green pepper. Cube the tofu.

Melt the margarine and fry the mushrooms and green pepper until soft. Stir in the flour and cook for 2-3 minutes. Add the milk very gradually, stirring constantly, bring it to the boil and continue stirring until thickened. Add the tofu, season to taste. Serve over toast or noodles.

Tofu Creole

1 lb (2 cups) firm tofu
2 small or 1 large onion
1 green pepper
2 oz (¼ cup) vegetable
  margarine
6 tablespoons wholemeal flour
2 14-oz tins tomatoes

2 teaspoons dried rosemary
2 teaspoons thyme
2 teaspoons oregano
Sea salt and freshly ground
  black pepper to taste
2 teaspoons raw sugar

Cube the tofu and deep-fry until browned. Drain well.

Finely chop the onion and green pepper. Sauté gently in the margarine for a few minutes, until soft. Stir in the flour and gradually add the tomatoes (chopping them coarsely as you do so) and the herbs and seasoning. Cook for 10-15 minutes until the sauce has thickened and the flavours have blended.

Add the tofu and cook for a further 5 minutes. Serve over cooked brown rice or pasta.

Tofu and green pepper bake

12 oz (1½ cups) firm tofu
2 medium-sized green peppers
1 clove garlic
1 lb tomatoes
1 teaspoon Tabasco sauce

4-6 tablespoons thick soya
  yogurt (see p. 10).
2 teaspoons paprika
Sea salt to taste

Put the tofu into a clean tea towel and squeeze until most of the moisture is gone; put the dry crumbly tofu into a mixing bowl.

Chop the green peppers finely. Mince the garlic. Chop the tomatoes.

Combine all of the ingredients with the tofu. Put into an

ovenproof dish, and bake at 400°F (200°C) Gas Mark 6, for 20 minutes.

Serve with wholemeal toast.

Baked tofu squares

6 oz (1 cup) short-grain brown
  rice
12 oz (1½ cups) firm tofu
1 cup soya milk
2 tablespoons soya flour
2 teaspoons sea salt

2 onions
2 tablespoons vegetable oil
2 carrots
1 15-oz tin kidney beans (or 5
  oz dried beans, cooked)
2 teaspoons dried rosemary

Cook the rice until tender. Set aside.

Mash the tofu. Add the soya milk, soya flour and salt and mix thoroughly.

Chop the onions finely. Sauté in the oil until tender but not brown. Add to the tofu mixture.

Grate the carrots finely. Drain the cooked beans. Add both to the tofu mixture along with the rice and rosemary. Mix thoroughly.

Turn the mixture into an oiled oven dish. Bake at 375°F (190°C) Gas Mark 5 for about 25 minutes, until the top is a light golden brown. Cool briefly before cutting it into squares.

Tofu casserole

3 oz (⅓ cup) vegetable
  margarine
4 tablespoons wholemeal flour

2 cups soya milk
12 oz-1 lb (1½-2 cups) firm
  tofu

<table>
<tr><td>

1 medium onion
1 green pepper
2 tablespoons vegetable oil
2 teaspoons curry powder

</td><td>

1 14-oz tin tomatoes
Sea salt to taste
2 oz (½ cup) dried wholemeal
  breadcrumbs

</td></tr>
</table>

Melt 2 oz of the margarine, stir in the flour, cook briefly for about 2 minutes, then slowly add the soya milk, stirring constantly, until it comes to the boil and thickens. Set aside.

Cube the tofu. Sauté in the remainder of the margarine until golden. Set aside.

Mince the onion and green pepper. Sauté in the vegetable oil until tender. Add the curry powder and stir briefly. Add the tomatoes and cook for about 10 minutes, stirring occasionally.

Add the tomato mixture and the tofu to the white sauce and mix thoroughly. Season to taste. Turn into an oiled casserole, and top with the breadcrumbs (additional margarine may be used to dot the top of the casserole if desired). Bake in a 350°F (180°C) Gas Mark 4 oven for about 15 minutes.

Vegetables topped with tofu custard

<table>
<tr><td>

1 lb frozen cut leaf spinach (or
  fresh spinach chopped after
  cooking)
12 oz hard white cabbage
2 leeks
4 tablespoons vegetable oil
4 small or 3 large courgettes
  (zucchini)
2 cloves garlic
Sea salt to taste

</td><td>

1¼-1½ lb (2½-3 cups) con-
  verted Japanese or medium
  tofu
3 tablespoons tahini
Juice of 1 lemon
3 teaspoons soya sauce
4 tablespoons soya yogurt
½ teaspoon cayenne (optional)
2 oz (1 cup) fresh wholemeal
  breadcrumbs

</td></tr>
</table>

Cook the spinach until tender.

Chop the cabbage and leeks. Add them to the oil in a wok or large frying pan. Stir-fry for 1-2 minutes, then cover, lower heat, and simmer for 4-5 minutes.

Chop the courgettes. Mince the garlic. Add to the wok, and stir-fry for 4-5 minutes longer. Add the spinach and salt to taste.

Combine the tofu, tahini, lemon juice, soya sauce, soya yogurt, and cayenne (if used) in a liquidizer and liquidize until smooth.

Put the vegetables into an oiled casserole, and pour the tofu mixture over them. Top with the breadcrumbs. Bake at 350°F (180°C) Gas Mark 4 for 35 minutes. Nice with boiled, roast or baked potatoes.

Gingered potato and tofu savoury

1½ lb potatoes	1 onion
2 oz (⅓ cup) sesame seeds	Small piece fresh ginger (1-2
8 oz (1 cup) firm tofu	inches)
½ cup soya milk	3 oz (½ cup) broken cashews
2 teaspoons cider vinegar	Sea salt to taste

Cook the potatoes. Cool and mash. Set aside.

Grind the sesame seeds. Set aside.

Put the tofu, soya milk and vinegar in a liquidizer and blend thoroughly.

Chop the onion and ginger, and add to the liquidizer. Blend until smooth.

Add the liquidizer mixture to the mashed potatoes, along with the ground sesame seeds and the cashew pieces. Add sea salt to taste and mix thoroughly.

Put into an oiled baking dish, and bake at 350°F (180°C) Gas Mark 4 for about an hour, until the top is lightly browned.

Tofu and spaghetti casserole

3 tablespoons vegetable
  margarine
2 tablespoons wholemeal flour
1 cup soya milk
½ teaspoon celery salt
1 teaspoon lemon juice
2 tablespoons chopped parsley
8 oz (1 cup) firm tofu

8 oz wholemeal spaghetti
6 oz mushrooms
1 small or ½ large green
  pepper
3 oz (½ cup) blanched slivered
  almonds
2 oz (1 cup) fresh breadcrumbs

Melt 2 tablespoons margarine; stir in the flour, then gradually add the milk, stirring constantly until thickened. Add the celery salt, lemon juice, and parsley. Crumble the tofu into it and stir well.

Cook the spaghetti until tender. Drain and set aside.

Chop the mushrooms. Sauté in the remainder of the margarine until tender. Mince the green pepper.

Add the mushrooms, green pepper and almonds to the creamed tofu mixture along with the cooked spaghetti. Mix thoroughly.

Place in an oiled casserole, top with the breadcrumbs and bake for about 20 minutes, or until top is lightly browned, at 375°F (190°C) Gas Mark 5.

Cauliflower terrine

1 large cauliflower
2 onions
10-12 oz (1¼-1½ cups)
   medium or converted
   Japanese tofu
4 tablespoons soya yogurt
4 tablespoons tahini
Juice of 1 lemon
2 tablespoons vegetable oil

6 oz (3 cups) fresh wholemeal
   breadcrumbs
Pinch grated nutmeg
6-8 tablespoons Smokey Snaps
   (available at health food
   stores)
Sea salt to taste
2 tablespoons minced parsley

Divide the cauliflower into flowerets and cook until tender. Drain and mash to a purée.

Chop the onions and sauté in the oil until tender but not brown.

Put the tofu, yogurt, tahini, and lemon juice in liquidizer and blend thoroughly.

Combine all of the ingredients, and put into an oiled casserole or loaf tin. Bake at 375°F (190°C) Gas Mark 5 for 1 hour. Serve with sauté or roast potatoes.

Sweet and sour cabbage

1 lb Savoy cabbage
1 onion
2 eating apples
8 oz (1 cup) firm tofu
Juice of 2 lemons
1½ tablespoons honey
½ cup soya yogurt
8 oz (1⅓ cups) bulghur wheat

1 tablespoon caraway seeds
2 tablespoons cider vinegar
2 tablespoons vegetable oil
2 oz (⅓ cup) raisins
Sea salt and freshly ground
   black pepper to taste
1 cup water
Pinch allspice

Shred the cabbage; chop the onion; peel and dice the apples.

Crumble the tofu into a large mixing bowl. Mix in all of the rest of the ingredients.

Place in an oiled casserole, and bake at 400°F (200°C) Gas Mark 6 for about 10 minutes, then lower to 350°F (180°C) Gas Mark 4 for a further 20 minutes.

Devilled tofu

12 oz (2 cups) brown rice
1 onion
1 large green pepper
2 sticks celery
4 oz (½ cup) vegetable
  margarine
4 oz mushrooms
Vegetable stock as required

Sea salt to taste
12 oz-1 lb (1½-2 cups) firm
  tofu
2 oz (½ cup) wholemeal flour
½ pint (1⅓ cups) water
4 tablespoons tomato purée
1-2 teaspoons made mustard

Cover the rice with boiling water; leave to soak for several hours. Drain and set aside.

Chop the onion, green pepper, and celery. Sauté in 1 oz of the margarine for about 5 minutes, stirring occasionally. Chop the mushrooms, and add them to the pan, along with the rice, and cook gently for 3-4 minutes. Add stock to cover and a little salt, bring to the boil, cover and simmer until tender.

Meanwhile, cube the tofu, and sauté in 1 oz of the margarine for a few minutes, turning it so that it is golden on all sides. Set aside.

Heat the remaining 2 oz margarine, and stir in the flour. Cook for about 2 minutes, then carefully add the water, stirring constantly. Bring to the boil, stirring as it thickens, and add the tomato purée and mustard.

Turn the rice mixture into a large serving dish (or 4 plates). Arrange the tofu cubes on top, and pour the sauce over the whole.

Savoury tofu triangles

10 oz (2½ cups) wholemeal
   flour
Sea salt to taste
5 oz (²/₃ cup) vegetable
   margarine
Water as required
8 oz fresh or frozen spinach

1 onion
2 tablespoons vegetable oil
4 oz mushrooms
3 tablespoons sesame seeds
1-2 tablespoons soya sauce
12 oz - 1 lb (1½-2 cups)
   medium or firm tofu

Put the flour in a mixing bowl, add a little salt. Mix the margarine in with the fingers, fork or pastry blender (N.B. with a firm margarine like Tomor it is easiest to use a pastry blender; with a soft margarine like Vitaquell a fork is best). Add enough water to make a pastry that is firm but not dry (it is better to have it a little sticky and use extra flour on the pastry board than to have it too dry – moister pastry at this stage makes for lighter pastry when cooked). Roll out and cut into squares (either 4 large, 8 medium, or 16 small ones).

To make the filling, steam the spinach until tender and chop it.

Chop the onion and sauté in the oil until tender.

Chop the mushrooms and add to the onion; sauté for a further 3-4 minutes.

Toast the sesame seeds. Add to the onions and mushroom along with the chopped spinach and the soya sauce.

Crumble the tofu into the spinach mixture.

Divide the filling evenly between the squares, and fold them up into triangles. Put them on lightly oiled baking sheets, prick the tops with a fork, and bake at 400°F (200°C) Gas Mark 6 for about 15 minutes, until golden. Serve immediately.

Savoury tofu and bulghur wheat

1 onion
4 sticks celery
2 tablespoons vegetable oil
1 tablespoons minced parsley
10 oz (1¼ cup) soft tofu or 1
  packet Morinaga Silken Tofu
¼ pint (⅔ cup) tomato juice
2 oz (1 cup) fresh wholemeal
  breadcrumbs

3 oz (¾ cup) walnuts
2 tablespoons Barbara's
  Organic Mashed Potatoes
  (available from health food
  stores)
1 teaspoon lemon juice
½ teaspoon thyme
8 oz (1⅓ cups) bulghur wheat
Sea salt to taste

Mince the onion and celery. Sauté in the oil until softened but not brown. Add the parsley.

Mash the tofu and mix with the tomato juice. Chop the nuts finely and add to the tofu mixture along with the breadcrumbs and dried mashed potatoes. Mix well.

Add the sautéed vegetables, the lemon juice, and the thyme, and mix thoroughly. Place the mixture in an oiled casserole. Bake at 350°F (180°C) Gas Mark 4 for 40 minutes.

Meanwhile, cook the bulghur wheat (use treble the amount of water to bulghur wheat) with a little sea salt, until tender.

Serve the tofu mixture over the wheat.

Quick and easy shepherd's pie

Mashed potatoes made from 1
 1b potatoes (or from
 Barbara's Organic Mashed
 Potatoes), soya milk and
 vegetable margarine, fla-
 voured with seasalt and
 freshly ground black pepper
 to taste

2 onions
4 tablespoons vegetable oil
3 tablespoons wholemeal flour
½ pint (1⅓ cups) water
1 tablespoon yeast extract (e.g.
 Marmite, Tastex, Yeastrel)
1 lb (2 cups) medium tofu

Chop the onions. Sauté in the oil until lightly browned.

Stir in the flour, then gradually add the water, stirring
constantly. When boiling and thickened, turn the heat down
and stir in the yeast extract.

Crumble the tofu into the saucepan, and mix well. Turn into
an oiled casserole and top with mashed potatoes.

Bake at 375°F (190°C) Gas Mark 5 for 15-20 minutes until top
is lightly browned.

Shepherd's pie with vegetables

1 onion
2 tablespoons vegetable oil
4 oz mushrooms
1 green pepper
2 carrots
1 14-oz tin tomatoes

1 bay leaf
½ teaspoon basil
1 lb (2 cups) medium or firm
 tofu
1 lb mashed potatoes (as
 above)

Chop the onion. Sauté in the oil until just tender.

Chop the mushrooms, green pepper and carrots. Add to the
onion and stir well.

Add the tomatoes, bay leaf and basil. Cover and simmer for

about 10 minutes. Crumble the tofu into the mixture and cook for a further 5 minutes.

Turn into a greased casserole, cover with mashed potatoes, and bake at 375°F (190°C) Gas Mark 5 for 15-20 minutes until lightly browned.

Grilled tofu with gravy

1 lb (2 cups) firm tofu
Soya sauce as required
10-12 slices buttered wholemeal toast

½ pint (1⅓ cups) water
3 tablespoons tahini
2 heaped teaspoons miso

Cut the tofu into slices about half an inch thick. Place the slices on a grill pan and brush the tops with a little soya sauce. Put under a medium grill (broiler) and grill for a few minutes. Turn the slices over, brush with a little more soya sauce, and grill the other side.

Meanwhile, bring the water to a boil. Put the tahini and miso into a liquidizer, add the water, and liquidize. Pour the sauce into a pan, bring to the boil over a low heat, simmer for a minute or two, then leave to rest for 2-3 minutes.

Place the tofu slices on the hot buttered toast, and spoon the gravy over them.

Cauliflower with tangy tomato/tofu topping

1 large cauliflower
1 large onion
1 oz (⅛ cup) vegetable
  margarine
1½ lb (3 cups) converted
  Japanese or medium tofu

1 tablespoon vegetable oil
3 teaspoons made mustard
3 tablespoons tomato purée
Sea salt and freshly ground
  black pepper
4 tablespoons chopped parsley

Break the cauliflower into flowerets. Steam in a little salted water until just tender. Drain.

Chop the onion. Sauté in the margarine until lightly browned.

Put the tofu, oil, mustard, tomato purée, and seasoning in a liquidizer and blend thoroughly. Stir the parsley and onion into this mixture.

Put the cauliflower into a greased oven dish. Pour the tofu mixture over the cauliflower.

Bake at 400°F (200°C) Gas Mark 6 for half an hour. Nice served with boiled, baked, or roast potatoes.

Tofu burgers

2 onions
3 sticks celery
2 tablespoons vegetable oil +
  additional for frying

1-1½ lb (2-3 cups) firm tofu
4 oz (1 cup) rolled oats
2 tablespoons soya sauce
1 teaspoon garlic salt

Mince the onions and celery. Sauté in the 2 tablespoons oil until lightly browned.

Crumble or mash the tofu in a bowl. Add the oats, soya

sauce, garlic salt, and the sautéed onion and celery. Mix well and knead with the hands. Form into burgers and shallow fry until browned on both sides.

Nice in a wholemeal bun with tomato ketchup, or alternatively serve with gravy and vegetables.

Tofu pot pie 1

8-10 oz wholemeal pastry
   (made from 8-10 oz wholemeal flour and 4-5 oz
   vegetable fat)
½ lb potatoes
2 small carrots
4 oz (¾ cup) fresh or frozen
   peas

4 oz tinned water chestnuts
1 lb (2 cups) firm tofu
4 tablespoons vegetable oil
Soya sauce as required
5 tablespoons wholemeal flour
1 pint (2⅔ cups) water
1 envelope Miso-Cup (available at health food stores)

Make the pastry and divide into two. Roll out the pastry for the bottom crust, put it into pie dish, prick with a fork, and bake at 400°F (200°C) Gas Mark 6 for 10 minutes.

Cut the potatoes and carrots into small cubes. Steam the carrots, potatoes and peas until just tender. Chop the water chestnuts coarsely.

Cube the tofu. Sauté in 1 tablespoon of the oil until browned. Put into a bowl and sprinkle with soya sauce; mix well.

Heat the remainder of the oil and add the flour. Gradually add the water, stirring constantly to avoid lumps. When the mixture has come to a boil add the Miso-Cup, stirring well.

Combine the steamed vegetables, gravy and tofu, and pour into partially baked pastry. Cover with pastry for top crust, and prick with a fork. Bake at 375°F (190°C) Gas Mark 5 for half an hour until crust is firm and lightly browned.

Tofu pot pie 2

Wholemeal pastry as above
1 lb (2 cups) firm tofu
2 oz (½ cup) wholemeal flour
  + 3 tablespoons
2 teaspoons garlic salt
6 tablespoons vegetable oil
2 small carrots
3 sticks celery
1 large onion

4 oz (¾ cup) fresh or frozen
  peas
¾ pint (2 cups) soya milk
Sea salt and freshly ground
  black pepper
1 teaspoon sage
½ teaspoon thyme
1 teaspoon paprika

Roll out and bake the bottom crust as in the recipe above.

Cube the tofu. Combine the 2 oz flour with the garlic salt. Toss the tofu cubes in this mixture.

Heat 4 tablespoons of the oil and add the coated tofu cubes. Stir well over medium heat until browned.

Chop the carrots, celery and onion and add to the tofu. Stir-fry until just tender. Add the peas and stir-fry for another minute or two.

Heat the remainder of the oil in a saucepan. Gradually stir in the 3 tablespoons flour, then the soya milk, stirring

constantly to avoid lumps. When this has come to the boil
add the salt and pepper, the sage and thyme and the
paprika.

Combine the gravy with the tofu/vegetable mixture, and
pour into the pie shell. Put the top crust over it, prick with a
fork, and bake at 370°F (190°C) Gas Mark 5 for about half an
hour.

Mushroom scramble

4 oz (½ cup) vegetable
  margarine
2 oz (½ cup) soya flour
1½-2 teaspoons yeast extract
1 onion

12 oz mushrooms
4 oz (¾ cup) fresh or frozen
  peas
8 oz (1 cup) firm tofu
Wholemeal toast as required

Melt 3 oz of the margarine. Remove from heat and stir in
soya flour and yeast extract. Spoon onto an oiled flat surface
and leave to cool, then chill in fridge.

Chop the onion and sauté in the remainder of the margarine
in a large frying pan until just tender.

Slice the mushrooms and add to the frying pan. Stir-fry 2-3
minutes, then add the peas and cook a few minutes longer.

Crumble the tofu into the frying pan and continue cooking
3-4 minutes longer.

Cut the chilled soya flour savoury into small pieces and add
to the frying pan, stirring well while it melts. Cook for a
further 2-3 minutes, then serve over wholemeal toast.

Tofu roast

1 onion
2 tablespoons vegetable oil
6 oz (1 cup) brown rice
6 oz (1 cup) red lentils
2 teaspoons yeast extract

2 oz (1 cup) fresh wholemeal
  breadcrumbs
8 oz (1 cup) medium or firm
  tofu
1 7-oz tin tomatoes

Chop the onion finely. Sauté in the oil until lightly browned.

Cook the rice and lentils until tender.

Add the cooked rice and lentils to the onion, along with the yeast extract and breadcrumbs. Crumble or mash the tofu and add to this mixture.

Liquidize the tomatoes and slowly mix in (the mixture should be moist but firm; do not add all the tomato if it looks like becoming too sloppy).

Put into a baking dish and bake at 350°F (180°C) Gas Mark 4 for about 40 minutes, until nicely browned. Serve with gravy and vegetables.

Leek and tofu quiche

2 large leeks
1 oz (⅛ cup) vegetable
  margarine
1-1½ lb (2-3 cups) medium or
  converted Japanese tofu
2 tablespoons lemon juice

1 teaspoon garlic salt
Freshly ground black pepper
Uncooked wholemeal pastry
  shell (made from 6-8 oz
  flour)

Wash and slice the leeks. Sauté in the margarine for 3-4 minutes.

Mash the tofu in a mixing bowl. Stir in the lemon juice, garlic salt and pepper. Add the sautéed leeks and mix in well.

Pour the filling into the pastry shell.

Bake at 400°F (200°C) Gas Mark 6 for about half an hour, until set and lightly browned. Nice with a green salad.

Mexican-style dishes

3
Mexican-style dishes

Tofu chilli with macaroni

2 onions
2 stalks celery
2 large green peppers
1 tablespoon olive oil
2 teaspoons Mexican chili
   seasoning
12 oz-1 lb (1½-2 cups) firm
   tofu

2 14-oz tins tomatoes
2 15-oz tins red kidney beans
   (or 10 oz dried beans which
   have been cooked until
   tender)
8-12 oz (2-3 cups) wholemeal
   macaroni
Sea salt to taste

Chop the onion, celery and green pepper. Heat the oil and sauté the onion until tender. Add the celery and green pepper and sauté for a further 2-3 minutes.

Add the tomatoes and chili seasoning; bring to the boil. Crumble the tofu and add to the pan. Turn the heat down to low and simmer for 10-15 minutes. Add the beans and simmer for a further 5 minutes.

Meanwhile, cook the macaroni until just tender. Drain well.

Toss the macaroni with the chilli mixture, turn into an oiled casserole, and bake at 350°F (175°C) Gas Mark 4, for 30-40 minutes.

Chili con 'queso'

2 onions
2 tablespoons vegetable oil
8 oz (1 cup) firm tofu
Mexican chili seasoning to
   taste (or, alternatively, use
   Sharwood's Concentrated
   Chili Maker and omit
   tomato purée and chili
   seasoning)

2 15-oz tins red kidney beans
   (or 10 oz dried beans which
   have been cooked until
   tender)
1 5-oz tin tomato purée
4 oz (2 cups) fresh wholemeal
   breadcrumbs
Water as required

Chop the onion and fry in the oil until lightly browned. Drain the beans.

Put the tofu into a clean tea towel and squeeze as much of the liquid out as possible so that the tofu is quite dry and crumbly.

Combine all of the ingredients, adding enough water to make the mixture stirrable. Bring to the boil over moderate heat, stirring constantly; turn heat to low and simmer for about 10 minutes.

Serve over brown rice, or as a filling for tacos.

Tofu enchiladas

5 oz (1¼ cup) wholemeal flour
3 oz (½ cup) maize flour
   (available from wholefood
   shops)
Pinch sea salt
5 tablespoons vegetable
   margarine
1 onion
2 cloves garlic

2 tablespoons vegetable oil
2 fresh chillies
1 7-oz tin tomatoes
2 tablespoons Mexican chili
   seasoning
Sea salt and freshly ground
   black pepper to taste
1 teaspoon cumin seeds
¼ teaspoon cayenne

1 5-oz tin tomato purée
¾ pint (2 cups) water
12 oz-1 lb (1½-2 cups) firm
  tofu
¼ pint (⅔ cup) soya yogurt
Pinch sea salt

½ teaspoon turmeric
¼ teaspoon paprika
2 oz button mushrooms
3-4 spring onions
Black olives as required

Combine the wheat and maize flours. Add the salt, then blend in the margarine. Add enough water to form a dough. Make small balls out of the dough (the size does not matter, as you can make either small or large tortillas), and roll them out with a rolling pin on a floured board. Place each circle on to an ungreased frying pan over a moderately high heat. When it begins to bubble, turn it over until the other side begins to bubble. Remove from heat and add the next circle; pile them on a plate ready for filling.

To make the salsa (sauce) first mince the onion and garlic. Sauté in the oil until softened.

Mince the chillies. Put the contents of the tin of tomatoes into a liquidizer and liquidize thoroughly.

Add the chillies, seasonings, tomato purée, liquidized tomatoes and water to the onions and garlic. Stir well. Bring to the boil, then simmer for about 20 minutes.

To make the filling mash the tofu and mix in the yogurt, salt, turmeric and paprika.

Mince the mushrooms and spring onions and add to the tofu mixture.

To assemble the dish, brush each tortilla with a little of the salsa, then spoon a little of the filling into the centre. Fold it over twice to form a rolled pancake shape. Cover the bottom of a baking sheet with a thin layer of salsa, and place each filled tortilla onto the sheet. When all the tortillas have been filled then spoon all of the remaining salsa over the top. If there is any filling left it can be used as decoration over the salsa. Finally, garnish with chopped olives.

Bake the enchiladas at 350°F (180°C) Gas Mark 4 for about half an hour. Serve immediately.

Tofu, rice and courgette enchiladas

6 oz (1 cup) brown rice
5 oz (1¼ cup) wholemeal flour
3 oz (½ cup) maize flour
Pinch sea salt
5 tablespoons vegetable
  margarine
1 14-oz tin tomatoes
Mexican chili seasoning to taste

1 large onion
1 clove garlic
2 tablespoons olive oil
2 courgettes (zucchini) – ½-¾
  lb
8-12 oz (1-1½ cups) firm tofu
2 tablespoons sesame seeds
2-3 spring onions

Cook the rice until tender and set aside.

Make tortillas as in the above recipe.

Put the tinned tomatoes into a liquidizer, add some chili seasoning, and blend thoroughly. Taste, and if the flavour is

not sufficiently strong stir in additional seasoning; if it is not spicey enough add a little cayenne or chilli powder. (The main constituents of Mexican chili seasoning are cumin, oregano and chilli powder; a combination of these will produce a 'Mexican' flavour.)

Chop the onion and mince the garlic. Sauté in the oil until tender.

Mince the courgettes. Add to the onion and garlic, along with the rice. Crumble the tofu into this mixture, adding a little salt to taste. Mix thoroughly.

Dip each tortilla into the puréed tomatoes, then place on a baking sheet which has been oiled with olive oil, and place a little filling on it. Roll up to close.

When all the tortillas have been filled spoon the remainder of the puréed tomatoes over the top and sprinkle with sesame seeds. Bake at 375°F (190°C) Gas Mark 5 for about half an hour.

Mince the spring onions and sprinkle over the enchiladas as garnish.

Burritos

¾ lb (3 cups) wholemeal flour
1 teaspoon sea salt
1 large onion
4 oz mushrooms
2 tablespoons vegetable oil
1 lb (2 cups) firm tofu
2 tablespoons soya sauce

3 teaspoons chili seasoning (or more to taste)
1 14-oz tin tomatoes
2 teaspoons ground cumin
½ teaspoon basil
2 teaspoons chopped parsley

Add the salt to the flour in a large bowl and add enough water to make a dough. Cover with a damp cloth and leave it for an hour or longer. Knead the dough, then pull off individual lumps of dough and roll each one out into a round, on a floured board. Heat a heavy frying pan, and cook each round for a few minutes on each side before removing from heat.

Chop the onion and mushrooms. Sauté in the oil until tender. Crumble in the tofu and sprinkle with the chili seasoning. Cook for about 10 minutes longer, stirring frequently. Add the soya sauce.

Put the tin of tomatoes into a liquidizer along with the cumin, basil and parsley. Blend thoroughly.

Add half the blended tomatoes to the tofu mixture, and stir well. Fill the burritos with this mixture and roll up. Place on an oiled baking sheet and top with the rest of the tomato sauce. Bake at 350°F (180°C) Gas Mark 4 for 20-30 minutes.

Tofu rancheros

1 14-oz tin tomatoes
1 onion
1 green pepper
1 red pepper
2 tablespoons vegetable oil

2 teaspoons Mexican chili
   seasoning
½ teaspoon turmeric
1 oz (¼ cup) soya flour
1 lb (2 cups) firm tofu

Drain the tinned tomatoes.

Chop the onion and peppers. Sauté in the oil until just tender. Add the seasoning, turmeric, and soya flour. Stir well, then slowly add the tomatoes. Bring to the boil, lower heat and simmer for about 5 minutes.

Put the tofu into a clean tea towel and squeeze well to extract the water.

Add the crumbled tofu to the tomato mixture. Heat for a minute or two, then serve over brown rice or tortillas.

Tofu tacos

1 onion
2 cloves garlic
3 tablespoons vegetable oil
1 tablespoon Mexican chili
   seasoning
2 tablespoons wholemeal flour
½ pint (1⅓ cups) water

2 tablespoons tomato purée
1 teaspoon yeast extract
8 oz (1 cup) firm tofu
Sea salt and freshly ground
   black pepper to taste
1 packet (12) tacos
Lettuce as required

Chop the onion. Crush the garlic. Sauté in the oil for a few minutes until tender. Stir in the chili seasoning and the flour. Add the water slowly, stirring constantly until it comes to the boil. Stir in the tomatoe purée and the yeast extract.

Crumble the tofu into the sauce. Simmer, uncovered, for about 10 minutes or until thick. Taste and add salt and pepper if required.

Meanwhile, heat the tacos according to the instructions on the packet.

Fill the individual taco shells with the tofu mixture and top with shredded lettuce. (N.B. This quantity is fine for a light lunch; for a full evening meal serve with Mexican rice and refried beans.)

Tamale pie

8 oz (1⅓ cups) maize meal
Sea salt to taste
1 onion
2 tablespoons vegetable oil
1 14-oz tin tomatoes
2 tablespoons wholemeal flour
A dozen black olives

½ teaspoon cayenne pepper
2 teaspoons dried basil
2 7-oz tins sweetcorn
8 oz (1 cup) firm tofu
2 tablespoons vegetable
  margarine

Combine the maize meal with a little salt, with 8 fluid ozs (1 US cup) cold water and ¾ pint (2 US cups) boiling water.

Bring it to the boil over direct heat, place over a saucepan of boiling water, then cover and leave to steam for about 15 minutes.

Chop the onion and sauté in the oil until tender.

Liquidize the tomatoes.

Add the flour to the onions and stir well. Slowly stir in the liquidized tomatoes. Bring to the boil, stirring constantly.

Mince the olives. Add to the tomato sauce along with the cayenne, basil and drained sweetcorn. Stir well.

Cut the tofu into small cubes. Sauté in the margarine until golden brown.

Spoon the maize meal mush into an oven dish, to cover the bottom and line the sides. Top with the tofu cubes. Pour the sweetcorn-tomato mixture over the top.

Bake at 350°F (180°C) Gas Mark 4 for 45 minutes. Serve with a green salad.

The Mediterranean

4
Italian-style dishes

Tofu risotto

12 oz (2 cups) brown rice
2 small onions
3 oz (⅓ cup) vegetable
  margarine
Vegetable stock or water as
  required
1 stick celery
1 green pepper
2 oz mushrooms

1 clove garlic
10-12 oz (1¼-1½ cups) firm
  tofu
2 tablespoons cider vinegar
2 oz Smokey Snaps (available
  at health food stores)
½ teaspoon basil
½ teaspoon marjoram

Cover the rice with boiling water and leave to soak for several hours. Drain.

Chop one of the onions. Melt half the margarine and sauté the onion until tender. Add the rice, cover with vegetable stock or water, bring to the boil, then simmer.

Meanwhile, chop the other onion, along with the celery, green pepper and mushrooms; crush the garlic. Dice the tofu. Melt the remainder of the margarine, and sauté the vegetable and tofu for a few minutes until tender. Add the vinegar, Smokey Snaps and herbs, cover and simmer for about 5 minutes.

When the rice is nearly ready add the vegetable and tofu mixture to it, stirring well, and continue cooking until the liquid is completely absorbed.

Tofu cacciatore

1 small onion
1 carrot
1 clove garlic
1 bay leaf
4 tablespoons vegetable oil
1 5 oz tin tomato purée
1½ cups water
1 lb (2 cups) firm tofu

8-12 oz (2-3 cups) wholemeal
   macaroni or pasta shells
1-2 oz (¼-½ cup) wholemeal
   flour
1 teaspoon basil
4 oz (¾ cup) fresh or frozen
   peas
Sea salt as required

Chop the onion, carrot and garlic, and sauté in half the oil, along with the bay leaf, for a few minutes. Add the tomato purée and water, bring to the boil and simmer for about 10 minutes.

Meanwhile, cook the macaroni or shells for 10-15 minutes in boiling salted water.

Cube the tofu. Dust lightly with the flour and basil and sauté in the remainder of the oil until lightly browned.

Add the tofu to the tomato sauce, along with the peas, and simmer until the peas are just tender.

Serve over the cooked macaroni or shells.

Tofu pizza

1 teaspoon raw sugar
¼ pint (⅔ cup) water at blood
   heat (a little more if
   required)
1 teaspoon dried yeast
1 teaspoon sea salt
8 oz (2 cups) wholemeal flour
1 onion

2 cloves garlic
2 tablespoons olive oil
1 14-oz tin tomatoes
2 tablespoons tomato purée
2 teaspoons oregano
1 teaspoon basil
Sea salt and freshly ground
   black pepper to taste

8-12 oz (1-1½ cups) firm or medium tofu
2-4 oz mushrooms
Small green pepper

Optional extras: sliced olives, capers, onions, artichoke hearts

Dissolve the sugar in half the water, then sprinkle in the yeast and mix with a fork. Cover and leave in a warm place for about 10 minutes, by which time it should be frothy. Add the salt to the flour, then pour in the yeast mixture, along with the remainder of the water. Add a little extra water if necessary to make a moist dough. Knead for 5 minutes. Roll out the dough and put in pizza pans. Cover and leave in a warm place for about half an hour.

Chop the onion. Mince the garlic. Sauté in the olive oil until tender. Add the tomatoes, purée and herbs; bring to the boil then simmer until thick, about half an hour. Season to taste.

Spread the sauce over the pizza base. (Any left over can be stored in the fridge).

Crumble the tofu over the sauce.

Mince the mushrooms; thinly slice the green pepper. Spread over the tofu along with any of the optional extras.

Bake at 450°F (230°C) Gas Mark 8 for 30-40 minutes.

Tofu calzone

1 onion
1-2 cloves garlic
2 tablespoons olive oil
1 carrot
2 sticks celery
1 small green pepper
2 oz mushrooms
4 tablespoons tomato purée
½ cup water

1 teaspoon basil
1 teaspoon oregano
8 oz (1 cup) firm or medium tofu
Sea salt to taste
4 oz (½ cup) vegetable margarine
8 oz (2 cups) wholemeal flour

Chop the onion; mince the garlic. Sauté in the olive oil for 3-4 minutes.

Chop the carrot, celery and green pepper and add to the saucepan. Chop the mushrooms and add to the pan when the other vegetables are nearly tender. Stir in the tomato purée, water, basil and oregano and bring to the boil. Cube the tofu and add to the pan. Lower heat and simmer for 5 minutes. Cool slightly.

Add the sea salt and margarine to the flour and mix well. Add enough water to make a dough, divide into four, and roll out into circles on a floured board.

Divide the filling into four, and spoon on to half of each circle. Fold the dough over to cover, and pinch it well to seal.

Bake at 375°F (190°C) Gas Mark 5 for 25-35 minutes until the crust is browned.

Aubergine tofuiana

1 14-oz tin tomatoes
1 onion

2 cloves garlic
3 teaspoons basil

1 tablespoon vegetable oil plus additional as required
Fine breadcrumbs or wholemeal flour as required

1-1½ lb aubergines (eggplants)
12 oz-1 lb (1½-2 cups) firm tofu

Liquidize the tin of tomatoes. Pour into a saucepan. Chop the onion and crush the garlic, add to the saucepan along with the basil and the tablespoon vegetable oil. Stir well, bring to the boil, then lower heat and simmer for about 20 minutes.

Slice the aubergines very thinly. Brush each slice with a little oil on both sides; then dip into fine breadcrumbs or flour. Put the slices under the grill and grill until tender, turning them over once. (Alternatively, shallow fry the slices in a little oil and drain well.)

Arrange half the aubergine slices in an oiled baking dish, crumble half the tofu over them, top with half the tomato sauce. Repeat the layers.

Bake at 350°F (180°C) Gas Mark 4 for 20-30 minutes.

Tagliatelle with creamy tofu sauce

12 (1½ cups) medium tofu
¼ pint (⅔ cup) soya yogurt
1 tablespoon tahini
2 heaped teaspoons miso

1 tablespoon lemon juice
12-14 oz wholemeal noodles
Freshly ground black pepper

Put the tofu, yogurt, tahini, miso and lemon juice in a liquidizer and blend well.

Cook the pasta until just tender and drain.

Toss the noodles with the tofu sauce, grind some black pepper over the top and serve at once.

Tofu lasagne*

1 large onion
1 clove garlic
2 14-oz tins tomatoes
2 tablespoons vegetable oil
1 tablespoon dried basil
2 teaspoons raw sugar

Sea salt and freshly ground
  black pepper to taste
8-10 oz wholemeal lasagne
12-14 oz (1½-1¾ cups)
  medium or firm tofu

Mince the onion and garlic. Combine the tomatoes in a saucepan with the onion, garlic, oil, basil and seasoning (including sugar). Cook for about half an hour until thickened.

Cook the lasagne in boiling salted water until tender (15-20 minutes). Drain well.

Mash the tofu.

Place alternative layers of lasagne, tofu and tomato sauce in an oven dish, starting with lasagne and ending with tomato sauce.

Bake at 375°F (190°C) Gas Mark 5 for 45 minutes.

*This recipe originally appeared in *The Vegetarian*, Sept/Oct 1982.

Spinach and mushroom lasagne

1 lb spinach
2 oz (¼ cup) vegetable margarine
1 teaspoon marjoram
Sea salt and freshly ground
  black pepper

12 oz-1 lb firm tofu
8 oz mushrooms
4 tablespoons wholemeal flour
½ pint (1⅓ cups) water
2 teaspoons soya sauce
8-10 oz wholemeal lasagne

Wash the spinach well, then cook it without additional water until it is just tender. Drain, reserving the liquid.

Chop the spinach coarsely, and while it is still warm mix in half the margarine. Season with marjoram, salt and pepper, then crumble the tofu into the spinach mixture and combine thoroughly.

Mince the mushrooms. Sauté in the remainder of the margarine until tender. Stir in the flour. Make up the spinach liquid with water up to half a pint, and stir in gradually until it thickens and boils. Mix in the soya sauce.

Place alternate layers of lasagne, spinach/tofu mixture, and mushroom sauce in an oven dish, ending with mushroom sauce on top.

Bake at 400°F (200°C) Gas Mark 6 for half an hour.

Courgette and mushroom lasagne with tofu topping

8-10 oz wholemeal lasagne
2 onions
2 tablespoons olive oil
2 cloves garlic
8-12 oz mushrooms
8-12 oz courgettes
12 oz tomatoes
1 tablespoon tomato purée
2 teaspoons oregano

1 teaspoon basil
Sea salt and freshly ground
 black pepper
1¼-1½ lb (2½-3 cups) con-
 verted Japanese or medium
 tofu
3 tablespoons tahini
Juice of 1 lemon
4 tablespoons soya yogurt

Cook the lasagne until tender, drain and rinse.

Chop the onions and sauté in the oil 3-4 minutes. Crush the garlic and add to the pan; cook for a couple of minutes longer.

Chop the mushrooms and courgettes and add to the onion

and garlic. Cook for 2-3 minutes longer.

Peel and chop the tomatoes. Add to the vegetables, along with the tomato purée and the herbs. Cover the pan and cook for 5-10 minutes. Season to taste.

Put the tofu, tahini, lemon juice, and yogurt into the liquidizer and blend thoroughly. Stir in salt and pepper to taste.

Layer the lasagne and vegetables in a baking dish. Pour the tofu mixture over the top. Bake at 350°F (180°C) Gas Mark 4 for 35-40 minutes, when it should be nicely browned on top.

Tofu ravioli

12 oz (3 cups) wholemeal (or 81%) flour
2 tablespoons soya flour
Pinch sea salt
¼ pint (¾ cup) warm water
8 oz (1 cup) firm tofu
½ teaspoon onion salt
½ teaspoon garlic salt
Freshly ground black pepper
Tomato sauce (for a home-made sauce use one of the recipes above; there are proprietary brand Italian tomato sauces available as well)

Mix the flour, soya flour and salt and add the water slowly to make a dough (do this slowly as different flours require slightly more or less liquid, and once the consistency of a dough has been reached no more water should be added). Knead well.

Mash the tofu in a mixing bowl. Stir in the onion and garlic salts and a little black pepper.

Roll the pastry out on a floured board, after dividing it into four or more sections. Cut out small squares. Place a little filling onto a square, cover with another square, and seal all round the edges with a fork to keep the filling inside.

Drop the squares into boiling salted water and cook for 10 minutes. Drain well, and serve with tomato sauce.

Spaghetti tofunese

1 large onion
2 carrots
2 sticks celery
4 oz mushrooms
3 tablespoons vegetable oil
1 14-oz tin tomatoes
8-10 oz (1-1¼ cups) firm tofu

2 teaspoons yeast extract
1 teaspoon chilli powder (optional)
2 tablespoons minced parsley
2 teaspoons basil
12 oz wholemeal spaghetti

Chop the onion, carrot, celery and mushrooms. Sauté in the oil for a few minutes.

Add the tin of tomatoes and bring to the boil. Crumble the tofu into the vegetable mixture. Stir in the yeast extract, chilli (if used), parsley and basil.

Simmer the mixture for about 20 minutes, uncovered. Serve over cooked spaghetti.

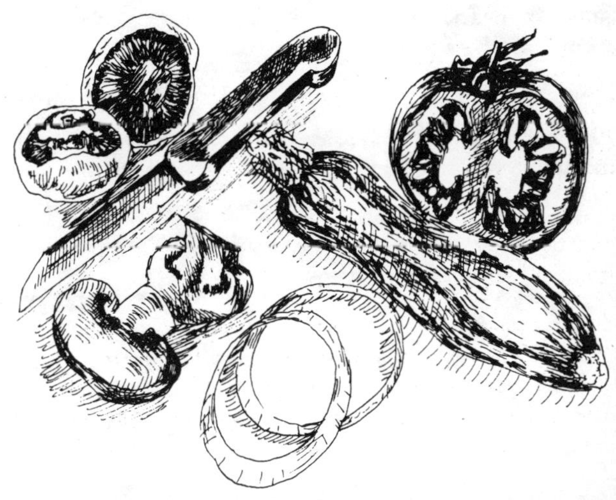

5
Other Mediterranean–style dishes

Valencia salad

12 oz (2 cups) long-grain brown rice
1 small tin (6¾ oz) pimento
2 or 3 slices onion
1 tablespoon minced parsley
Sea salt to taste

1 cup virgin olive oil
4 tablespoons cider vinegar
1 14-oz tin artichoke hearts
8 oz (1 cup) firm tofu
1 14-oz tin asparagus

Cook rice until tender. Chop the pimento and add to the rice.

Add the onion slices, parsley and salt to the olive oil. Leave to stand half an hour. Remove the onion slices and mix in the vinegar.

Stir half the vinaigrette sauce into the rice and pimento.

Chop the artichoke hearts coarsely. Marinate in the remainder of the vinaigrette.

Cube the tofu.

When ready to serve add the artichoke with dressing to the rice, along with the cubes of tofu. Decorate with the asparagus.

Iranian carrots and nuts with saffron pilav

12 oz (2 cups) long-grain
  brown rice
4 cardamom pods
2 onions
3 oz (⅓ cup) vegetable margarine
3 1-inch pieces cinnamon stick
4 whole cloves
Sea salt to taste
¼ teaspoon crushed saffron
  threads (soaked in a little
  hot water for at least 15
  minutes)

8-12 oz carrots
5 dates
1 tablespoon raisins or sultanas
1 tablespoon cider vinegar
2 tablespoons lemon juice
8-12 oz (1-1½ cups) medium
  or firm tofu
½ teaspoon turmeric
A little freshly ground black
  pepper
2 tablespoons blanched
  slivered almonds

Cover rice with boiling water and leave to soak for several hours. Drain.

To make pilav, remove the seeds from the cardamom pods and chop one onion. Melt 2 oz margarine and add the cardamom seeds, cinnamon and cloves. Fry, stirring constantly, for 2 minutes. Add the onion and fry, stirring occasionally, for several minutes, until golden brown.

Add the rice and cook over low heat for 3-4 minutes. Cover with water, add the salt and the saffron water; bring to the boil, then lower the heat and simmer for about 15-20 minutes until tender.

Meanwhile, peel and thinly slice the carrots crossways. Melt the remainder of the margarine, add the carrots and sauté for a few minutes, stirring frequently.

Chop the other onion. Add to the carrots and sauté until soft.

Chop the dates. Add to the carrot mixture, along with the raisins, vinegar and lemon juice. Cover the saucepan, lower the heat, and simmer for about 15-20 minutes.

Meanwhile, mash the tofu along with the turmeric, pepper and a little salt.

When the carrots are tender, add the mashed tofu and stir well until tofu is thoroughly heated.

Sprinkle with the almonds and serve over the saffron rice.

Spanish nomlette

12 oz potatoes	1½ lb (3 cups) firm or medium
2 tomatoes	tofu
2 tinned pimentos	2 oz (½ cup) wholemeal flour
2 small onions	1½ teaspoons baking powder
3 tablespoons olive oil	Sea salt and freshly ground
4 tablespoons cooked peas	black pepper to taste

Cook the potatoes. Dice them. Peel and chop the tomatoes. Chop the pimentos.

Chop the onions. Sauté in the oil for 2-3 minutes, then add the tomatoes, pimentos, potatoes and peas. Fry for a few minutes, stirring.

Put 4 oz of the tofu into a liquidizer and blend until creamy (if necessary add a little water).

In a large mixing bowl mash the remainder of the tofu. Add the blended tofu, the flour, and the baking powder, and mix well.

Add the vegetable mixture to the tofu mixture, and mix well, adding seasoning.

Form the mixture into 4 patties, and place on an oiled baking sheet. Bake for about half an hour at 325°F (170°C) Gas Mark 3, then flip the patties over and cook for a further 15 minutes.

Greek-style pizza

1 large onion
4 tablespoons olive oil
12 oz fresh spinach
12 oz (1½ cups) firm tofu
1 clove garlic
12 black olives

Sea salt and freshly ground
  black pepper
1 tablespoon oregano
Wholemeal pizza dough (for
  ingredients and method see
  under Italian-style dishes, p. 54)

Chop the onion. Sauté in the oil until just tender.

Chop the spinach. Add to the onion, cover the pan for 3-4 minutes, until the spinach is limp.

Mash the tofu. Mince the garlic and olives. Add to the onion and spinach along with salt and pepper to taste, and the oregano.

Roll out the pizza crust. Bake at 400°F (200°C) Gas Mark 6 for

about 5 minutes. Remove from oven and top with tofu/-spinach mixture. Return to oven and bake for 15-20 minutes until the crust is fully cooked.

Arroz con tofu

12 oz (2 cups) long-grain
  brown rice
1 large onion
1 large or 2 small green
  peppers
2 cloves garlic
4 tablespoons olive oil
1 14-oz tin tomatoes
½ pint (1⅓ cups) vegetable
  stock or water

½ teaspoon crushed saffron
Sea salt and freshly ground
  black pepper
1 lb (2 cups) firm tofu
1 oz (⅛ cup) vegetable margarine
1 7½-oz tin pimentos
4 oz (¾ cup) fresh or frozen
  peas

Cover the rice with boiling water and leave to soak for several hours.

Chop the onion and green pepper; crush the garlic. Sauté in the olive oil until just tender.

Drain the rice and add to the saucepan, along with the tomatoes and stock. Bring to the boil, then stir in the saffron and seasoning. Lower heat and simmer.

Cube the tofu. Sauté in the margarine until golden. Add to the rice mixture and stir well.

Chop the pimento. When the rice is tender and the liquid nearly absorbed (15-20 minutes), add the pimento and peas. Cook for a further 3-4 minutes before serving.

Spanish tofu spaghetti

12 oz wholemeal spaghetti
2 onions
2 green peppers
3 tablespoons olive oil
2 teaspoons turmeric

12 oz-1 lb (1½-2 cups) firm
   tofu
2 teaspoons garlic salt
Freshly ground black pepper

Cook the spaghetti until just tender. Drain.

Chop the onions and green peppers. Sauté in the olive oil in a frying pan until tender and lightly browned.

Mash the tofu. Add the turmeric and garlic salt and pepper to taste, and mix well.

Add the tofu to the frying pan and stir until thoroughly heated.

Stir in the cooked spaghetti and fry for a few minutes longer before serving.

Asia

6
Indian-style dishes

Curried tofu

2 onions
1 clove garlic
2 oz (¼ cup) vegetable
  margarine
2 teaspoons coriander seeds
2 teaspoons black peppercorns
1 teaspoons cumin seeds
1 teaspoon whole cardamoms
¼ inch piece of cinnamon
  stick

1 teaspoon ground cloves
2 teaspoons turmeric
2 teaspoons wholemeal flour
1-1½ lb (2-3 cups) firm tofu
½ pint (1⅓ cups) vegetable
  stock
1 teaspoon raw sugar
Sea salt to taste
Juice of ½ lemon

Chop the onions and mince the garlic. Melt the margarine and sauté the onions and garlic until just tender.

Grind the coriander, pepper and cumin; peel the cardamons and grind. Add all of the spices, including cinnamon stick, to the onions and garlic, along with the flour, and stir well.

Cube the tofu and add it to the above. Stir well to thoroughly coat with the spices. Add the vegetable stock and bring to the boil. Simmer for 10 minutes.

Add the salt and sugar and simmer for a further 10 minutes. Finally, add the lemon juice just before serving.

Tofu pilau

12 oz (2 cups) long-grain
  brown rice
2 onions
2 oz (¼ cup) vegetable margarine
2 bay leaves
Sea salt to taste

12 oz-1 lb (1½-2 cups) firm
  tofu
2 teaspoons turmeric
½ teaspoon chilli powder
2 teaspoons garam masala
2 teaspoons lemon juice
2 tomatoes

Cover the rice with boiling water and leave to soak for several hours. Drain well.

Chop the onions and sauté in half the margarine for 3–4 minutes. Add the rice, the bay leaves and salt; cover with boiling water and simmer until nearly tender.

Cube the tofu. Melt the remainder of the margarine and add the turmeric, chilli powder and garam masala; fry for 2-3 minutes and add the lemon juice. Stir the tofu cubes into the pan and leave to cook gently for 3-4 minutes before removing from the heat.

About 5 minutes before the rice is ready (normally about 15 minutes) add the tofu mixture and stir well. Continue simmering until rice is tender and water absorbed.

Before serving, remove bay leaves and garnish with sliced raw tomatoes.

Saag (spinach) tofu

8-12 oz (1-1½ cups) firm tofu
1 teaspoon garam masala
1 teaspoon sea salt
Small piece fresh ginger (about
  1 inch)

3 cloves garlic
1 fresh green chilli
1-1½ lb spinach
3 tablespoons vegetable oil
4 tablespoons soya milk

Cube the tofu and deep-fry until golden brown. While still hot sprinkle with the garam masala and with ½ teaspoon salt. Set aside.

Chop the ginger, garlic and chilli roughly and put into a liquidizer or food processor along with 4 tablespoons water. Blend until smooth.

Coarsely chop the spinach.

Heat the oil in a saucepan, and add the ginger-garlic-chilli paste. Stir for about 30 seconds, then add the spinach and remainder of salt. Stir for a minute, then cover the saucepan and leave to simmer for 5-10 minutes (there should be enough water clinging to the spinach leaves to cook them, but if necessary add a tablespoon or two of water).

Then put in the tofu cubes and soya milk, stir gently, and leave to simmer for a further 5-10 minutes, stirring once or twice during this period.

Serve over plain brown rice, pilau rice, or with an Indian bread.

Scrambled tofu with spicy tomato topping

1 lb ripe tomatoes
4 spring onions
1 fresh green chilli
2 cloves garlic
Small piece fresh ginger (about ¼ inch)
2 tablespoons whole coriander seeds
3 tablespoons vegetable oil
1½ teaspoons black mustard seeds

½ teaspoon sea salt
1-1½ lb (2-3 cups) firm or Chinese tofu
4 teaspoons turmeric
2 tablespoons soya sauce
1 oz (2 tablespoons) vegetable margarine (plus additional for spreading)
8-12 slices wholemeal toast

Peel and chop the tomatoes. Mince the spring onions, chilli

and garlic; grate the ginger finely. Grind the coriander seeds.

Heat the oil in a saucepan. When hot, put in the mustard seeds. After a few seconds, when they have begun to pop, add the spring onions and garlic. Stir for about 3 minutes, then add the tomatoes, ginger, coriander, and chilli. Stir and cook over medium heat for 6-8 minutes, then add salt.

Mash the tofu. Mix in the turmeric and soya sauce. Heat the margarine in a frying pan, and fry the tofu in it, stirring and turning over frequently for about 5 minutes.

Serve the scrambled tofu over buttered wholemeal toast, topped with the tomato mixture.

Rice with tofu and peas

12 oz (2 cups) long-grain
  brown rice
1 fresh green chilli
4 tablespoons vegetable oil
  (plus oil for deep-frying)
2 bay leaves
1-inch piece cinnamon stick

5 whole cardamom pods
1 teaspoon ground cumin seed
Sea salt to taste
8-12 oz (1-1½ cups) medium
  or firm tofu
8 oz (1½ cups) fresh or frozen
  peas

Cover the rice with boiling water, leave to soak for several hours and drain.

Mince the chilli.

Heat the oil and put in the bay leaves, cinnamon, cardamoms, cumin, and chilli. Stir once, then add the rice, stirring over a medium heat for 3-5 minutes. Cover with water and add a little salt; bring to the boil, then cover and simmer.

Meanwhile, cut the tofu into small cubes and deep-fry until golden brown.

When the rice is very nearly ready, add the peas, and cook until just tender. Add the tofu cubes and stir well so that they are thoroughly heated before serving.

Spaghetti madras

8 oz (1 cup) firm tofu
Vegetable oil for deep-frying
1 onion
2 oz (¼ cup) vegetable marg-
    arine
12 oz cabbage
2-3 tomatoes

1 teaspoon turmeric
¼ teaspoon dry mustard
Pinch cayenne
Small tin (5 oz) tomato purée
¼ pint (⅔ cup) water
8 oz wholemeal spaghetti
1 oz (⅙ cup) seedless raisins

Cube and deep-fry the tofu until golden. Set aside.

Chop the onion and sauté in 1 oz of the margarine until just tender. Shred the cabbage; skin and chop the tomatoes. Add to the onions along with the turmeric, mustard and cayenne. Combine the tomato purée and water and add to the vegetables, along with the deep-fried tofu cubes. Cook, covered, for about 10 minutes.

Meanwhile, cook the spaghetti until tender. Blanch the raisins in a little boiling water. Drain the spaghetti and toss with the remaining 1 oz margarine.

Pour the sauce over the spaghetti and sprinkle with blanched raisins.

Tofu patia with vermicelli

2 onions	1 teaspoon ground cumin
1 green pepper	1 lb (2 cups) firm tofu
4 tablespoons vegetable oil	4 teaspoons turmeric
3 cloves garlic	1 14-oz tin tomatoes
2 fresh green chillies	4 tablespoons water
1 teaspoon finely chopped	Sea salt to taste
fresh ginger	12 oz vermicelli

Slice the onions thinly. Chop the pepper finely.

Heat the oil in a heavy frying pan. Sauté the onion and green pepper for 3-5 minutes until the onion is just tender.

Mince the garlic and de-seeded chillies. Add to the frying pan, along with the ginger and cumin. Stir for another minute.

Cube the tofu. Toss with the turmeric, then add to the pan, stirring well. Add the tomatoes and water and stir again. Simmer until the mixture is fairly thick, adding a little salt if required.

Boil the vermicelli until just tender, and serve with the tofu mixture poured over.

Tofu, potatoes and cauliflower

1 small head cauliflower	Sea salt to taste
2 medium-sized potatoes	½ teaspoon whole fenugreek
Small piece (about 1 inch)	seeds
fresh ginger	Small stick (about 1 inch)
3-4 cloves garlic	cinnamon
4 tablespoons water	2 fresh green chillies
2 onions	2 tomatoes
2 tablespoons vegetable oil	2 teaspoons curry powder

1 oz (⅛ cup) vegetable margarine
2 tablespoons lemon juice
1 teaspoon garam masala

2 oz creamed coconut + 1½
  cups hot water
8-12 oz (1-1½ cups) firm tofu

Break the cauliflower into flowerets and cook for about 1 minute, then drain and rinse with cold water. Set aside.

Cook the potatoes; cool them, peel if desired, and cut into thick slices.

Put peeled ginger and garlic in a liquidizer or food processor with the 4 tablespoons water, and blend. Chop the onions finely.

Heat the oil in a heavy frying pan. Put in the fenugreek seeds and the cinnamon stick, and stir. Then add the onions and sauté for 2-3 minutes.

Mince the chillies. Add to the frying pan along with the ginger/garlic mixture. Stir and fry for another minute.

Peel and chop the tomatoes. Add to the frying pan along with the curry powder, and fry for a further 2 minutes.

Combine the creamed coconut and hot water in a liquidizer (or even a glass jar) to make coconut milk. Add to the above mixture, and simmer for about 5 minutes. Add the cauliflower and a little salt, and simmer for a further 5 minutes, with the pan covered.

Cut the tofu into large cubes, and sauté in the margarine until golden.

Add to the cauliflower mixture along with the potatoes and the lemon juice. Simmer for another 5 minutes.

Sprinkle the garam masala over it before serving. Nice over brown rice.

Vegetable kheema

2 large or 4 small tomatoes
3 fresh chillies
3 cloves garlic
½ -inch piece fresh ginger
3 whole cloves
Seeds of 3 cardamoms
8 whole peppercorns
2 teaspoons cumin seeds

½ teaspoon chilli powder
3 onions
4 tablespoons vegetable oil
1 cauliflower (1½-2 lb)
½ teaspoon turmeric
¼ pint (⅔ cup) water
6 oz (¾ cup) firm tofu
Sea salt to taste

Peel and chop the tomatoes. Put in a liquidizer, along with minced chillies, garlic and ginger, whole cloves, cardamom seeds, peppercorns, cumin, and chilli powder. Blend very thoroughly.

Chop the onions. Sauté in the oil until lightly browned. Add the tomato mixture and continue to cook for 3-4 minutes.

Grate the cauliflower. Add to the saucepan along with the turmeric and water. Bring to the boil, then lower heat and simmer for about 10 minutes.

Uncover the saucepan and crumble the tofu into it. Stir well, then add salt to taste. Simmer, uncovered, for 3-4 minutes.

Nice served with chapatis or other Indian bread.

Dahl with tofu

2 onions
2-3 cloves garlic
2 oz (¼ cup) vegetable
   margarine
8 whole cloves
½-inch cinnamon stick
2 teaspoons cumin seeds

2 teaspoons coriander seeds
1 teaspoon poppy seeds
Seeds of 4 cardamoms
1 teaspoon chilli powder
2 teaspoons turmeric
8 oz (1 cup) red lentils
1½ pints (3¾ cups) water

8 oz (1 cup) firm tofu
1 oz creamed coconut

Sea salt to taste
Brown rice as required

Chop the onions. Mince the garlic. Sauté in half of the margarine until lightly browned.

Put the cloves, cinnamon, cumin, coriander, poppy seeds and cardamom seeds into a liquidizer or coffee grinder and grind thoroughly.

Stir the ground spices into the onion and garlic, along with the chilli powder and turmeric. Stir well and cook for a minute or two. Stir in the lentils. Add the water, bring to the boil, then lower heat and simmer for 15-20 minutes.

Cube the tofu. Sauté in the remainder of the margarine until golden.

When the lentils have turned into a thick purée stir in the creamed coconut, the tofu cubes, and salt to taste.

Serve over brown rice, with mango chutney.

Tofu and peas korma

1 lb (2 cups) firm tofu
Oil for deep-frying
2 large or 4 small tomatoes
1 oz (¼ cup) cashew pieces
1-inch piece fresh ginger
4 cloves garlic
2 large onions
2 oz (¼ cup) vegetable
   margarine
2 cinnamon sticks
2 bay leaves

4 cloves
1 teaspoon chilli powder
½ pint (1⅓ cup) water
½ pint (1⅓ cup) soya yogurt
2 teaspoons cumin seeds
1 teaspoon coriander
2 teaspoons garam masala
4 oz (¾ cup) fresh or frozen
   peas
1 teaspoon raw sugar
Sea salt to taste

Divide the tofu into two halves. Cut one half into small cubes and deep-fry until golden.

Peel and chop the tomatoes. Put in liquidizer, along with cashew pieces, chopped ginger and garlic. Liquidize thoroughly.

Grate the onions coarsely. Sauté them in the margarine until lightly browned. Lower the heat, stir in the cinnamon, bay leaves and cloves, and cook 3-4 minutes longer. Stir in the chilli powder, then add the water, puréed tomato mixture and the yogurt. Bring to the boil.

Grind the cumin and coriander, and stir into the mixture, along with the garam masala. Simmer for a few minutes.

Add the deep-fried tofu cubes and the peas and cook for a further 2-3 minutes.

Crumble the remainder of the tofu into the saucepan, along with the sugar, and salt to taste. Heat thoroughly before serving. Nice over brown rice.

7
Chinese-style dishes

Peking noodles with tofu

5 or 6 dried mushrooms
1 clove garlic
2½ tablespoons sesame oil
   (available in Chinese shops)
3 tablespoons hoisin sauce
   (ditto)

2-3 tablespoons soya sauce
12 oz-1 lb (1½-2 cups) firm
   tofu
2 tablespoons vegetable oil
12 oz-1 lb Chinese noodles
3-6 spring onions

Cover the mushrooms with water and leave to soak for at least half an hour. Drain them, reserving the soaking liquid, and cut into thin strips.

Mince the garlic. Combine with ½ tablespoon sesame oil, hoisin sauce, and soya sauce. Set aside.

Cube the tofu. Heat the vegetable oil in a wok or heavy frying pan. Add the tofu and stir-fry 2-3 minutes. Add the mushrooms as well as the sesame oil-hoisin sauce mixture and about a teaspoon or two of the reserved mushroom liquid. Reduce the heat and cook for 2-3 minutes.

Meanwhile, cook the noodles until tender and drain. Toss with the 2 tablespoons sesame oil. Mince the spring onion.

Mix the noodles with the tofu mixture, garnish with the spring onions and serve immediately.

Quick and easy tofu lo mein

8 oz (1 cup) firm tofu
1-2 tablespoons soya sauce
1-2 tablespoons cornflour
12 oz thin Chinese noodles
Sesame oil
1 15-oz tin bamboo shoots

1 small bunch spring onions
2 tablespoons vegetable oil
8 oz (4 cups) fresh bean-
  sprouts
Sea salt to taste

Dice the tofu. Sprinkie with the soya sauce and then with the cornflour, and toss well. Set aside.

Boil the noodles until just tender, drain well and run cold water over them. Toss with 1 tablespoon sesame oil and set aside.

Drain the tin of bamboo shoots and slice thinly. Chop the spring onions.

Heat the vegetable oil in a wok or frying pan. Add the tofu and stir-fry for 2-3 minutes. Add the bamboo shoots, lower the heat to medium, and stir-fry for 1-2 minutes. Add the noodles, raise the heat, stirring constantly, allowing some of the noodles to become browned.

Add the bean sprouts and stir-fry for 2 minutes. Add the salt, spring onions, and additional sesame oil to taste, and mix thoroughly. Serve immediately.

Tofu with almonds

1 packet (3½ oz) dried-frozen
  or ½ lb (1 cup) frozen tofu
4 tablespoons vegetable oil
4 oz (1 cup) blanched whole
  almonds
1 green pepper

1 carrot
Small tin bamboo shoots
1 onion
1½ tablespoons cornflour
2 teaspoons raw sugar
  (optional)

1½ tablespoons soya sauce
2 teaspoons cider vinegar

½ pint (1⅓ cups) water
Cooked brown rice

Rehydrate the tofu and cut each piece into halves (or smaller pieces).

Heat 1 tablespoon oil and fry the almonds until golden.

Chop the vegetables.

Heat 2 tablespoons oil and sauté the onion until transparent. Add the remainder of the oil and the tofu and vegetables and cook, stirring occasionally, for a few minutes.

Blend the cornflour, sugar (if used), soya sauce, and vinegar with the water, and pour over the tofu and vegetable mixture. Bring to the boil, stirring constantly until it thickens.

Add the almonds and serve over brown rice (with additional soya sauce if required).

Tofu fried rice

12 oz (2 cups) short-grain
  brown rice
1 lb (2 cups) firm tofu
1 medium onion
8 oz mushrooms
8 oz (1½ cups) frozen peas
Soya sauce

1 small tin bamboo shoots
  (sliced)
4 tablespoons Smokey Snaps
  (available at health food
  stores)
4 tablespoons vegetable oil
  (plus oil for deep-frying)

Cook rice.

Divide the tofu in half. Cube and deep-fry one half. Set aside.

Chop the onion and stir-fry in a wok or frying pan in the 4 tablespoons of oil for 3-4 minutes.

Chop the mushrooms, add them to the onion, and stir-fry a further 3-4 minutes. Add the peas, bamboo shoots, deep-fried tofu cubes, and Smokey Snaps. Stir-fry 2-3 minutes longer.

Crumble the other half of the tofu into the vegetables, and stir-fry for about 2 minutes. Add the rice and soya sauce to taste, stir-fry the whole mixture until well heated and serve at once.

Tofu with spinach

1¼-1½ lb (2½-3 cups) Chinese
  or medium tofu
5 tablespoons vegetable oil
4 small or 2 large leeks
1 lb fresh spinach
1 tablespoon cider vinegar

1 tablespoon soya sauce
¼-½ teaspoon Tabasco sauce
1 tablespoon yellow bean
  paste (available from
  Chinese shops)

Cut the tofu into small dice. Heat 3 tablespoons of the oil in a wok or frying pan and when hot add the tofu pieces. Stir-fry for about 2 minutes, then remove from the pan onto kitchen paper to drain.

Chop the leeks and spinach. Add the rest of the oil to the wok and add the vegetables. Stir-fry for about 3 minutes, covering the wok between stirs if desired.

Stir in the vinegar, soya sauce, Tabasco sauce and yellow bean paste. Add the tofu pieces and stir gently.

Serve over brown rice or noodles.

Szechwan tofu with peanut sauce

1 medium carrot
1-inch piece fresh ginger
1 tablespoon vegetable oil
1 lb (2 cups) medium or
   Chinese tofu
1 tablespoon cider vinegar

1 spring onion
2 tablespoons peanut butter
¼ teaspoon cayenne
2 tablespoons sesame oil
1 tablespoon honey

Slice the carrot into matchsticks. Mince the ginger. Heat the vegetable oil in a wok or frying pan, add the carrot and ginger, and stir-fry for 2-3 minutes.

Cut the tofu into small pieces. Add to the wok, along with the vinegar. Cover and leave to simmer for about 3 minutes.

Mince the spring onion and add to the wok. Turn the heat off and leave, covered, for a minute or two.

Meanwhile, combine the peanut butter, cayenne, sesame oil and honey in a small bowl, stirring gently until smooth.

Add the peanut sauce to the tofu mixture, and mix well.

Serve over brown rice.

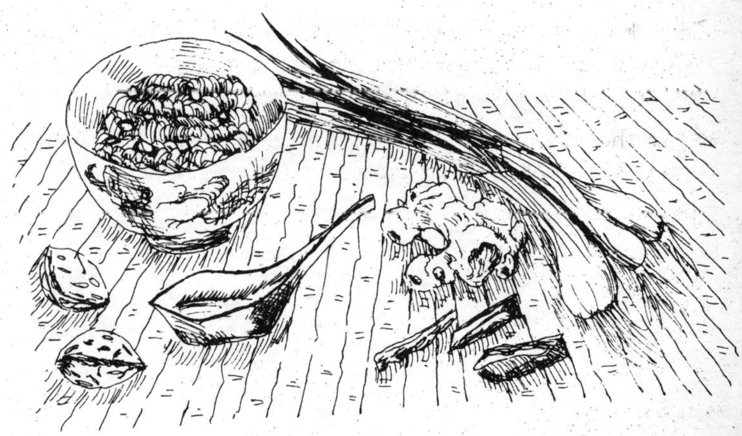

Moo goo gai pan

2 onions
4 sticks celery
4 oz (2 cups) mushrooms
4 oz (2 cups) fresh bean-
  sprouts
1 green or red pepper
1 small tin water chestnuts
4-6 oz Chinese cabbage
12 oz-1 lb (1½-2 cups)
  Chinese, medium or firm
  tofu

3 tablespoons soya sauce
1-2 oz fresh ginger
2-3 cloves garlic
6 tablespoons vegetable oil
2 tablespoons arrowroot
¾ pt (2 cups) water
4 tablespoons cider vinegar
Sea salt to taste
Cooked brown rice

Slice the onions thinly. Chop the celery and mushrooms; cut the green or red pepper into slivers. Slice the water chestnuts and cabbage.

Dice the tofu. Sprinkle the soya sauce over the tofu, put into a grill pan, and grill under a medium heat for a few minutes on each side.

Mince the garlic and ginger. Sauté in 4 tablespoons of the oil over medium heat for about 3 minutes.

Mix the arrowroot with 2 tablespoons of the water, the vinegar, and the salt. Pour the remainder of the water over the ginger and garlic, and bring to the boil. Turn down to a

simmer, then slowly stir in the arrowroot mixture until thickened.

Heat the remainder of the oil in a wok or large frying pan. Add the onion, celery, mushrooms and pepper, and stir-fry for about 5 minutes. Add the Chinese cabbage, water chestnuts and beansprouts, and stir-fry for a further 3-5 minutes.

Add the tofu to the vegetable mixture and stir well. Then pour over the ginger/garlic sauce, and stir well over a low heat until well mixed.

Serve over brown rice.

Mushroom-smothered tofu

1¼-1½ lb (2½-3 cups) Chinese tofu
16 dried mushrooms (available at Chinese shops)
2 spring onions
1-inch piece fresh ginger

4 tablespoons vegetable oil
1 tablespoon cider vinegar
3 tablespoons soya sauce
1 teaspoon raw sugar
1 tablespoon sesame oil
Brown rice as required

Quarter each square of tofu; then cut each of these into two triangles. Halve these as well. Set aside.

Cover mushrooms with boiling water and leave to soak for an hour or more. Drain them (reserving the liquid) and squeeze gently. Remove stalks and slice mushrooms.

Mince spring onions and ginger. Heat the oil in a wok or frying pan. Add the spring onions and ginger and stir-fry for a minute. Add the vinegar, soya sauce, sugar and mushroom liquid (if less than ⅓ pint (¾ cup) then add water). Bring to the boil and add mushrooms and tofu.

Turn gently a few times. Lower heat, cover and simmer for about 10 minutes, turning once halfway through. By the end of the cooking time there should be little or no liquid remaining. Add the sesame oil and serve over brown rice.

Tofu foo yung*

1 onion	1 teaspoon turmeric
2 spring onions	1 teaspoon sea salt (or more to taste)
8 oz mushrooms	
2 tablespoons vegetable oil	1 tablespoon soya sauce
12-14 oz (1½-1¾ cup) firm, medium or Chinese tofu	8 oz bean sprouts
	Brown rice as required

Mince the onion, spring onions and mushrooms. Heat the oil in a frying pan and stir-fry until tender.

Mash the tofu, mix well with the turmeric and add to the frying pan, stirring well. Add the salt and soya sauce while stirring. Finally, add the bean sprouts and continue stir-frying until they are just wilted.

Serve over brown rice, with additional soya sauce if desired.

*This recipe originally appeared in *The Vegetarian*, Sept/Oct 1982.

Steamed tofu and carrots with hot tahini sauce

1-1¼ lb (2-2½ cups) Chinese tofu	3 teaspoons cider vinegar
8 oz carrots	3 teaspoons Chinese chilli sauce
4-5 tablespoons tahini	4 tablespoons water
4-5 tablespoons sesame oil	2 teaspoons raw sugar
3-4 tablespoons soya sauce	Brown rice as required

Cube the tofu. Slice the carrots diagonally. Place them in a vegetable steamer and steam for a few minutes until the carrots are just tender.

Combine the tahini, sesame oil, soya sauce, vinegar, chilli sauce, water and sugar in a small saucepan. Heat over a gentle flame, stirring constantly until smooth.

Serve the tofu and carrots over the rice, topped with the sauce.

Braised tofu

1-1½ lb (2-3 cups) Chinese or medium tofu
3 tablespoons vegetable oil
1 tablespoon finely grated fresh ginger
2 teaspoons raw sugar

3 tablespoons soya sauce
¼ pint (⅔ cup) water
Brown rice as required
Stir-fried mixed vegetables if desired

Put the squares of tofu (Chinese tofu is sold in squares usually weighing 3-4 oz, so if using another type of tofu cut into squares of that weight) into a saucepan and cover with water, to about 2 inches above the tofu. Bring to the boil over medium heat and simmer for half an hour. Cool, then drain. Cut each square into eight cubes and press on them gently to remove excess water.

Heat the oil in a pan over medium heat and add the ginger and tofu cubes. Stir-fry for a minute or two, then stir in the sugar, soya sauce and ¼ pint water. Cover and bring to the boil, then lower the heat and simmer for about an hour, basting occasionally, until most or all the liquid has been absorbed.

Serve over brown rice, with stir-fried mixed vegetables if desired.

Sweet and sour tofu balls

1 lb (2 cups) Chinese tofu
½ teaspoon sea salt
2 tablespoons wholemeal flour
Vegetable oil for deep-frying
4 oz fresh or tinned pineapple
1 green pepper
2 spring onions

5 tablespoons cider vinegar
3-4 tablespoons raw sugar
2-3 tablespoons soya sauce
1 tablespoon cornflour
    dissolved in ⅓ pint (¾ cup)
    pineapple juice
Brown rice as required

Wrap the tofu in a clean tea towel or kitchen paper and leave to drain for half an hour or more. Put the drained tofu into a mixing bowl, mash well, and stir in salt and flour. Form into small balls and deep-fry until golden brown. Drain well.

Chop the pineapple if necessary. Slice the green pepper into thin slivers. Mince the spring onions.

Put the vinegar, sugar, soya sauce, and cornflour/juice mixture into a wok or saucepan, and bring to the boil gently, stirring constantly until thickened.

Add the tofu balls, pineapple, pepper and spring onions, and simmer to heat through for 2-3 minutes.

Serve immediately over brown rice.

Tofu with red chilli sauce

1 leek
2 cloves garlic
2 tablespoons vegetable oil
4 oz mushrooms
½-1 teaspoon chilli powder
¼ pint (⅔ cup) water
1 tablespoon cider vinegar
2 tablespoons tomato ketchup

1 tablespoon soya sauce
1-1½ lb (2-3 cups) Chinese tofu
1 tablespoon cornflour dissolved in 3 tablespoons water
2 spring onions
Brown rice as required

Chop the leek finely. Mince the garlic. Heat the oil in a wok or frying pan and add the leek and garlic. Stir-fry for about 30 seconds.

Chop the mushrooms and add to the wok. Stir-fry for another minute or two.

Add the chilli powder, water, vinegar, ketchup and soya sauce, bring to the boil and cook for another minute.

Cube the tofu and add to the wok. Stir in the dissolved cornflour and stir until thickened.

Mince the spring onions.

Serve the tofu in chilli sauce over brown rice, garnished with the minced spring onion.

Szechwan-style tofu

1 lb (2 cups) Chinese tofu
3 tablespoons vegetable oil
2 green peppers
2 leeks
2 fresh chillies
1-1½ teaspoons chilli powder
1 tablespoon cider vinegar

1 teaspoon raw sugar
2-3 tablespoons yellow bean
   paste (available at Chinese
   shops)
Brown rice as required
2 teaspoons sesame oil

Cut the tofu into small cubes.

Heat 2 tablespoons of the oil in a wok or frying pan, and stir-fry the tofu cubes for 2-3 minutes. Remove from wok and drain.

Slice the green peppers into strips. Chop the leeks. Mince the seeded chillies.

Heat the remaining tablespoon of oil and add the vegetables. Stir-fry for about 3 minutes. Add the chilli powder, vinegar, sugar and yellow bean paste and mix well.

Return the tofu cubes to the wok and stir-fry the mixture for about 3 minutes longer.

Serve over brown rice, sprinkled with sesame oil.

(NB. Soya sauce may be added to this dish if desired, but yellow bean paste is so salty I have never found it necessary.)

Ma po tofu with noodles

2 small leeks
4 cloves garlic
2 tablespoons vegetable oil
1-1½ lb (2-3 cups) Chinese tofu
½ pint (1⅓ cups) water or vegetable stock
2 teaspoons Chinese chilli sauce
2 tablespoons soya sauce

1 teaspoon freshly ground black pepper
3 oz Smokey Snaps (available from health food stores)
12 oz Chinese noodles
1 tablespoon cornflour dissolved in 2 tablespoons water
1 tablespoon sesame oil

Chop the leeks and garlic finely. Heat the vegetable oil in a wok or frying pan, and stir-fry the leeks and garlic for 3-4 minutes.

Cut the tofu into small cubes. Stir into the leek and garlic. Add the water or stock, chilli sauce, soya sauce, pepper, and Smokey Snaps. Bring to the boil, then lower heat and simmer for about 10 minutes.

Cook the noodles until just tender and drain.

Add the cornflour mixture to the tofu mixture and stir well until thickened. Serve over the noodles, and sprinkle with the sesame oil before serving.

8
Other Far Eastern-style dishes (Indonesian, Malaysian, Burmese, Japanese)

Fried tofu with peanuts

1 lb (2 cups) Chinese tofu
Vegetable oil for deep-frying
2 cloves garlic
6 oz (1 cup) plain dry-roasted
   peanuts (available at some
   wholefood shops or wash
   salt off ordinary roasted
   peanuts)
2 tablespoons soya sauce
2 tablespoons cider vinegar or
   lemon juice

½ teaspoon Sambal Oelek
   (available at delicatessens)
1 teaspoon dark Muscavado
   sugar
½ cup coconut milk (or just
   under ½ cup water and ½
   oz creamed coconut)
4 oz white cabbage
3 oz (1½ cups) fresh beansprouts
4 spring onions

Cube the tofu. Deep-fry until golden brown and drain.

Crush the garlic and sauté in 1 tablespoon of the oil over low heat, stirring constantly, for 1-2 minutes.

Grind half the peanuts and add to the garlic, along with the soya sauce, vinegar, Sambal, and sugar. Stir until well mixed. Gradually add coconut milk (or water and creamed coconut) and stir until the sauce is a thick pouring consistency.

Shred the cabbage finely.

Put the tofu on serving dish, cover with the cabbage and then with the bean sprouts. Spoon the sauce over.

Mince the spring onions. Sprinkle over the top of the sauce along with the whole peanuts.

Gado-gado

1 lb (2 cups) firm tofu
3 tablespoons vegetable oil
1 onion
2 or 3 cloves garlic
½ pint (1⅓ cups) hot water
8 oz (1 cup) crunchy peanut
  butter
2 teaspoons dark Muscavado
  sugar
1 tablespoon grated fresh
  ginger

Juice and rind of 1 lemon
1 teaspoon tabasco sauce (or 1
  tablespoon finely minced
  fresh chillies)
1 cup coconut milk (or 1-2 oz
  creamed coconut diluted
  with ¾ cup hot water)
8 oz shredded cabbage
8 oz green beans
8 oz fresh beansprouts
¼ cucumber

Cube the tofu and sauté in 2 tablespoons of the oil until golden brown. Remove from heat.

Chop the onion and garlic finely and fry in the remaining oil until lightly browned.

Stir the hot water and peanut butter into the onions and garlic and stir over low heat until the peanut butter has melted. Add the sugar, tabasco sauce, lemon, ginger and coconut milk, stirring well until thoroughly blended.

Blanch the cabbage and green beans (the beansprouts may be blanched or served raw). Slice the cucumber. Arrange the vegetables on a plate, top with the tofu cubes and pour the sauce over the whole.

Malay vermicelli

2 teaspoons whole coriander seeds
Seeds from 2 cardamom pods
2 teaspoons cumin seeds
2 teaspoons turmeric
½ teaspoon ground cinnamon
Pinch ground cloves
2 teaspoons ground fenugreek
4 onions
4 tomatoes
12 oz-1 lb (1½-2 cups) firm tofu

2 oz (¼ cup) vegetable margarine
3 cloves garlic
2 teaspoons sea salt
2 teaspoons chilli powder
1 tablespoon minced fresh ginger
¼ pint (⅔ cup) water
Juice of 1 lemon
12 oz vermicelli
A little fresh parsley

Heat all of the spices in a dry heavy frying pan until aromatic, then grind in a mortar or blender until pulverized.

Chop the onions coarsely, then put in liquidizer and blend. Peel and chop the tomatoes. Dice the tofu.

Melt the margarine, add the puréed onion and sauté, stirring, until lightly browned. Add the tomatoes and fry for a minute or two, then add the diced tofu and stir-fry for a further 2-3 minutes.

Crush the garlic and add to the saucepan, along with the salt, chilli powder, ginger and the spice mixture, stirring well.

Add a little of the water and simmer over a low heat for a few minutes. Then add the rest of the water and the lemon juice, stirring, and leave to simmer for about 5 minutes longer.

Boil the vermicelli until just tender and drain.

Toss the tofu mixture with the vermicelli, and garnish with the parsley.

Fried tofu with soya sauce

12oz-1 lb (1½-2 cups) Chinese
  or medium tofu
Oil for deep frying
4 spring onions
4 oz (2 cups) fresh bean-
  sprouts
1 onion

1 teaspoon Sambal Oelek
  (available at some delicatessens) or 1 fresh chilli
1 clove garlic
¼ cup soya sauce
1 tablespoon Muscavado or
  other dark raw sugar

Dice the tofu and deep-fry until golden. Drain, then arrange on a dish.

Mince the spring onions.

Cover the tofu with the beansprouts and sprinkle with the spring onions.

Chop the onion coarsely. Seed and chop the chilli if used. Chop the garlic. Put soya sauce, sugar, onion, garlic and Sambal or chilli into the liquidizer and blend thoroughly.

Pour the soya sauce mixture over the rest and serve.

Burmese-style kung lo mein

8 oz (1 cup) firm tofu
4 garlic cloves
4 tablespoons vegetable oil (+
  additional for deep-frying)
1 teaspoon sesame oil
8 oz spinach

8 oz Chinese cabbage
4 spring onions
2 fresh chillies
1½-2 tablespoons soya sauce
12 oz Chinese noodles

Cube the tofu and deep-fry until golden. Set aside.

Mince the garlic. Heat the oils in a wok or large frying pan until very hot. Drop in the garlic pieces and fry until brown, being careful not to let them burn. Remove and drain on kitchen towels.

Chop the spinach and Chinese cabbage coarsely. Chop the spring onions and seeded chillies finely. Put the vegetables into the wok and stir-fry for about 3 minutes, until the spinach has wilted. Add the deep-fried tofu and the soya sauce and mix well.

Boil the noodles until just tender and drain. Toss with the tofu and vegetable mixture. Sprinkle with the crisp garlic bits and serve.

Japanese mixed vegetables and tofu

6 oz (¾ cup) Chinese tofu
1 small aubergine (eggplant)
Sea salt as required
1 clove garlic
1 onion
2 tablespoons vegetable oil (+
  oil for deep-frying)
4 oz cabbage
4 oz broccoli
4 oz green beans

1 green pepper
2 sticks celery
2 oz mushrooms
½ small tin sliced bamboo
  shoots
¼ pt (¾ cup) water
1 teaspoon freshly ground
  black pepper
2 tablespoons soya sauce
Cooked brown rice

Cube and deep-fry the tofu. Set aside.

Slice the aubergine thinly. Salt the slices; leave with a weight on them for about half an hour, then rinse and pat dry.

Crush the garlic. Slice the onion thinly. Heat the oil in a wok or large frying pan, and sauté the onion and garlic until lightly browned.

Chop the cabbage coarsely. Cut the broccoli into flowerets. Slice the beans, green pepper, celery, and mushrooms. Add these vegetables to the onion and garlic, along with the aubergine and bamboo shoots, and stir-fry for 3-5 minutes. Add the water, pepper and soya sauce, bring to the boil, then reduce heat and simmer for 5-10 minutes. Add the tofu and simmer for a further 5-10 minutes.

Serve over brown rice.

Tofu brochettes

8 oz (1 cup) firm tofu
6-8 oz courgettes (zuccini)
4-6 oz carrots
6-8 oz mushrooms
2-3 tablespoons sesame oil
1-2 tablespoons + 1-2 tea-
    spoons curry powder
Sea salt and freshly ground
    black pepper

1 large onion
3 tablespoons vegetable oil
½ (1⅓ cups) pint water
2 tablespoons peanut butter
Juice of ½ lemon
1 teaspoon yeast extract
2 teaspoons raw sugar
Brown rice as required

Drain and cube the tofu. Slice the courgettes and carrots. Remove stalks from mushrooms and clean. Sprinkle sesame oil, 1-2 teaspoons curry powder, and salt and pepper over the vegetables and tofu and mix well. Leave to marinate for about an hour, turning occasionally.

Chop the onion. Sauté in the vegetable oil until just brown. Add the water and bring to the boil. Add the peanut butter, 1-2 tablespoons curry powder, lemon juice, yeast extract and sugar. Leave to cool briefly, then put in the liquidizer and blend thoroughly. Return to saucepan and heat gently, stirring constantly.

Thread the tofu and vegetables on to skewers and place under a hot grill. Grill until lightly browned and sizzling, turning occasionally.

Remove the vegetables and tofu from the skewers and serve on brown rice with the sauce poured over.

Desserts

9
Desserts

Roshmalay (an Indian sweet)

1 lb (2 cups) medium or firm tofu
1½ cups soya milk (if using powdered or tinned variety add less than the required amount of water so that it is slightly thicker than usual)
1 oz (⅛ cup) vegetable margarine

6 whole cardamoms
2 oz (⅓ cup) slivered almonds
⅛ teaspoon freshly ground nutmeg
4-6 oz (¾-1 cup) raw sugar
2 teaspoons rosewater
½ teaspoon vanilla essence
8 tablespoons (just under ¼ cup) water

Put the tofu into a clean tea towel and squeeze until as much as possible of the liquid has been removed. Place the tofu in a mixing bowl and knead briefly. Form into small balls about the size of walnuts and set aside.

In a saucepan bring the soya milk and margarine to a boil. Remove the seeds from the cardamoms, grind them and add to the saucepan, along with the almonds, nutmeg, and half the sugar. Turn the heat down to fairly low and simmer, uncovered, for 10-15 minutes. Remove from heat, add rosewater and vanilla essence, and leave to cool.

In a small saucepan combine the water and rest of the sugar, bring to the boil, and cook uncovered over medium heat for about 15 minutes. Dip the tofu balls into the syrup and place on a plate to cool.

Put the tofu balls into serving bowls, pour the milk mixture over them, and chill thoroughly until ready to serve.

Apricot triangles

4 oz (½ cup) vegetable margarine
8 oz (1 cup) firm tofu
4-5 oz (1-1¼ cups) 81% (or 85%) wholemeal flour

¼ teaspoon sea salt
Raw sugar apricot jam as required
Finely ground raw sugar as required

Combine the margarine, tofu and salt. Using a wooden spoon blend thoroughly.

Add the flour and knead until a soft dough is formed. Cover and chill.

Roll the dough out and cut into small squares. In the centre of each square put about a teaspoon of apricot jam. Fold the dough over to form a triangle and press the edges together to seal. Prick with a fork, and bake on an oiled sheet at 375°F (190°C) Gas Mark 5 for half an hour.

Sprinkle the tops with finely ground raw sugar and serve warm.

Cheesecake

8 oz granola (e.g. Jordan's Crunchy Cereal or similar)
3-4 oz (⅓-½ cup) vegetable margarine
⅓ pint (¾ cup) soya milk
1¼ lb (2½ cups) firm tofu
8 tablespoons (½ cup) vegetable oil

1 tablespoon vanilla essence
1 teaspoon almond extract
2 teaspoons arrowroot
Fruit topping (e.g. fresh strawberries or cherries, stewed fruit thickened with a little arrowroot, 'runny' raw sugar jam, etc.)

Grind the granola until very fine. Melt the margarine and mix in the granola crumbs. Spread in a greased flan tin and bake at 350°F (180°C) Gas Mark 4 for 5 minutes.

Put the soya milk, tofu, oil, vanilla essence, almond extract and arrowroot into liquidizer and blend thoroughly until smooth (this will probably need to be done in two or three batches). Pour over the crumb crust.

Bake at 350°F (180°C) Gas Mark 4 for 20 minutes. Remove from heat and leave to cool. Top with fruit topping and chill in fridge before serving.

Pashka (Russian cream) I

8-12 oz (1-1½ cups) firm tofu
2 oz (¼ cup) vegetable
  margarine
4-5 tablespoons soya yogurt
2 oz (⅓ cup) raw sugar

2 oz (⅓ cup) ground almonds
2 oz mixed candied peel,
  finely chopped
3 oz (½ cup) raisins
½ teaspoon vanilla essence

Put the tofu into a clean tea towel and squeeze well to get rid of as much liquid as possible.

Put the squeezed tofu into a mixing bowl, and cream the margarine into it. Mix in all the rest of the ingredients.

Spoon the mixture into one large or four small serving dishes, press down firmly, cover and chill in fridge for several hours before serving.

Pashka II

8-12 oz (1-1½ cups) firm tofu
2 oz (⅓ cup) raw sugar
2 oz (⅓ cup) ground almonds
4-5 teaspoons soya yogurt

Juice and rind of 1 lemon
3 oz (½ cup) sultanas, raisins
   or a mixture

Put the tofu into a clean tea towel and squeeze well to get rid of as much liquid as possible.

Combine with all the other ingredients and serve.

Tofu pie

½ teaspoon powdered agar-
   agar
½ cup water
6 oz (1 cup) broken cashews
8 oz (1 cup) firm or medium
   tofu
½ pint (1⅓ cups) soya yogurt
4 teaspoons lemon juice

2 teaspoons vanilla essence
4 tablespoons raw sugar
1 pre-baked wholemeal pastry
   shell (made from 4-6 oz
   flour and 2-3 oz vegetable
   margarine)
Fresh strawberries

Dissolve the agar in the water, bring to the boil and simmer for a minute.

Put the cashews in the liquidizer and grind until fine. Add the water and agar, along with the tofu, yogurt, lemon juice, vanilla essence, and sugar. Blend thoroughly.

Pour into the pie shell. Chill thoroughly. Top with strawberries before serving.

Honeyed tofu and yogurt pie

8-12 oz (1-1½ cups) firm tofu
½ pint (1⅓ cups) soya yogurt
4 tablespoons honey
1 teaspoon vanilla essence

1 pre-baked wholemeal pastry shell
Fresh fruit (e.g. strawberries, bananas, peach, kiwi fruit)

Put the tofu into a clean tea towel and squeeze until the liquid has been extracted. Put into a mixing bowl and add the yogurt, honey and vanilla. Beat well.

Spoon the tofu mixture into the baked pie shell, cover and chill for several hours.

When ready to serve top with sliced fresh fruit.

Coconut custard pie

6 oz vegetarian Digestive
  biscuits
2 oz (¼ cup) vegetable
  margarine
12 oz (1½ cups) converted
  Japanese or medium tofu

4 tablespoons vegetable oil
1 teaspoon vanilla essence
¼ teaspoon sea salt
3-4 oz (½-¾ cup) raw sugar
3½ oz (1¼ cups) desiccated
  coconut

Grind the biscuit crumbs finely (or crush with a rolling pin). Melt the margarine and mix with the crumbs. Turn them into a greased flan tin and pat down firmly. Bake at 375°F (190°C) Gas Mark 5 for 15 minutes.

Put the tofu, oil, vanilla, salt and sugar into the liquidizer and blend thoroughly. Stir in 3 oz of the coconut.

Pour the mixture into the crumb shell and bake at 350°F (180°C) Gas Mark 4 for 15 minutes. Sprinkle the top with the remainder of the coconut and bake for about 5 minutes longer. Cool, then chill before serving.

Raspberry tofu cheesecake

1½ oz (½ cup) rolled oats
½ oz (⅙ cup) desiccated
  coconut
½ oz (⅛ cup) vegetable
  margarine
12 oz (1½ cups) firm tofu
2 tablespoons soya yogurt
2 tablespoons raw sugar
Juice and rind of ½ orange

½ teaspoon vanilla essence
2 teaspoons tahini
Pinch sea salt
2-3 tablespoons honey
4 tablespoons water
⅛ teaspoon powdered agar-
  agar
4 oz fresh or frozen
  raspberries

Mix the oats and coconut together. Spread the margarine over the bottom of a flan tin, then sprinkle the oat-coconut mixture over it. Set aside.

Combine the tofu, yogurt, sugar, orange juice and rind, vanilla, tahini and salt in a liquidizer. Blend thoroughly. Pour into the flan case.

Melt the honey in the water over a medium heat and dissolve the agar powder in it. Bring to the boil then simmer for about a minute. Remove from heat and stir in raspberries. Pour over the tofu mixture in the flan tin.

Bake at 350°F (180°C) Gas Mark 4 for 35 minutes.

Chill for several hours before serving.

Apricot cream

4-6 oz dried apricots
8-12 oz (1-1½ cups) medium
  or firm tofu
2-3 teaspoons lemon juice

4 tablespoons raw sugar
2 tablespoons soya yogurt
3-4 tablespoons flaked
  almonds

Soak the apricots for several hours or steam until tender (apricots which have been cooked will give a creamier texture; apricots which have simply been soaked will give a cream with a 'chewier' texture).

Combine all the ingredients except the almonds in a liquidizer and blend thoroughly.

Pour into dessert dishes and top with almonds. Serve chilled.

Strawberry cream

1 lb fresh strawberries
12 oz (1½ cups) medium or
   firm tofu

Juice of 1 lemon
4-6 tablespoons raw sugar
¼ teaspoon vanilla essence

Leave aside a few of the nicest strawberries. Put all the rest in the liquidizer, along with the other ingredients, and liquidize thoroughly.

Decorate with the strawberries which have been set aside. Serve chilled.

Chocolate-topped pie

3-4 oz wholemeal pastry
12 oz (1½ cups) converted
   Japanese or medium tofu
3 oz (½ cup) raw sugar
1½ teaspoons vanilla essence

1 tablespoon vegetable oil
1½ oz plain chocolate
4 tablespoons water
1 tablespoon cornflour

Roll the pastry out, put it into a flan dish, prick it with a fork, and bake at 425°F (220°C) Gas Mark 7 for 10 minutes. Remove from oven.

Put the tofu, 2½ oz of the sugar, 1 teaspoon of the vanilla, and the oil in a liquidizer and blend thoroughly. Pour into partially baked pie shell, and bake at 350°F (180°C) Gas Mark 4 for half an hour.

In a basin or small saucepan over a saucepan of boiling water, melt the chocolate. Stir in the remaining sugar and vanilla. Dissolve the cornflour in the water, and stir into the chocolate. Continue stirring until mixture has thickened.

Spoon the chocolate mixture over the baked pie. Leave to cool, then chill until ready to serve.

Sweet tofu fritters

8 oz (1 cup) firm tofu
2 oz (½ cup) wholemeal flour
1 tablespoon honey
Vegetable oil for deep-frying
8 oz apricot jam

2 teaspoons orange flower
  water (available at specialist
  delicatessens and food halls)
4 tablespoons water

Mash the tofu in a mixing bowl. Stir in the flour, the honey, and 1 teaspoon of orange flower water.

Form the tofu mixture into walnut-sized mounds and deep-fry until golden brown. Drain and keep warm.

Heat the apricot jam in a small saucepan. Add the water and other teaspoon orange flower water. Bring to the boil.

Serve the fritters warm with the hot sauce poured over them.

Vanilla ice cream

8 oz (1 cup) medium or converted Japanese tofu
2 teaspoons vanilla essence

2 tablespoons vegetable oil
2-3 oz (⅓-½ cup) raw sugar
⅓ pint (¾ cup) soya milk

Combine all the ingredients in a liquidizer and blend thoroughly.

Pour into a suitable container and put in freezer. Stir frequently as it is freezing to avoid crystallization. Transfer the ice cream from the freezer to the fridge 10-15 minutes before serving.

Index